LOVE MAGIC

LOVE MAGIC

Sally Morningstar

 A GODSFIELD BOOK

This book is dedicated to the memory of

my beloved father – Cliff Owen

ACKNOWLEDGMENTS

To the Shining Ones, I offer my deepest thanks. To David, my partner, for so much support and care. To my son Laurence, wizard of the gentle way, for his undying patience with my busyness; to Rachael Clyne, friend and spiritual sister, for generously sharing contacts and creativity; to Cazzie for her wonderful friendship and inspiring craftwork; to Rag for his magical beauty; to Chris Hynam from Incense Magic; to Collette Prideux Brune, who is always wise and helpful – and a true example of unconditional friendship; to my stepmother – Virginia Owen from Court End Catering – for guiding me with her natural gift for the fruits and seeds of the earth; to my mother who helped with Laurence and gave "sensible motherly advice" at those times when writing took over my universe. Many others molded and carved my moments during the writing of this book, including Shane the Green Man! All of them loved and thanked with big hugs and smiles. I am truly blessed.

Library of Congress Cataloging-in-Publication
Data Available

10 9 8 7 6 5 4 3 2

Published in 2000 by
Sterling Publishing Company, Inc.
387 Park Avenue South, New York, N.Y. 10016
© 2000 Godsfield Press
Text © 2000 Sally Morningstar

Sally Morningstar asserts the moral right to be
identified as the author of this work.

Distributed in Canada by Sterling Publishing
c/o Canadian Manda Group, One Atlantic Avenue, Suite 105, Toronto,
Ontario, Canada M6K 3E7
Distributed in Australia by Capricorn Link (Australia) Pty Ltd, P O. Box 6651,
Baulkham Hills, Business Centre, NSW 2153, Australia

Printed and bound in China

Sterling ISBN 0-8069-2781-X

CONTENTS

ABOUT THIS BOOK

MARCH
TO MAY

Love Magic will show you how to connect to the magical world so that you can deepen your own connection to the wisdom of the heart. It shows you how to work with magic in a beautifully simple and yet creative way, allowing space for your own unique magical expression. For example, when making a wand, you are guided in the basic steps and then given the option to use whichever totems, charms, and objects you wish so that your wand is personal to you.

With all magical working, it is important to cleanse, bless, and consecrate anything that you intend to use. This ceremonial act connects you to the power that lies dormant within each object, awakening its potency. Your respect and dedication leads to cooperation from the energetic world of magic.

In seeking love it is important to remember that High Magic does not manipulate the free will of any sentient life. For this reason, when working a magical spell or making a potion, be careful to keep an open mind and an open heart, naming no names. In this way, your call for love is free to go where it needs to go, to be heard by the person who will most meet your needs. If you try to manipulate another, this may well backfire on you and the result will not be what you wanted or needed at all.

The same principle applies when making a love potion. It is for your personal use only and should not be "slipped into someone's tea." That kind of magic is not in the spirit of love and beauty, and may well be problematic, raising issues you would rather have left alone. All potions and spells are for the greater good of your own self. If someone else speaks of wanting to try a spell or potion of their own free will – that is fine.

Throughout this book, you will find suggestions on how to reconnect with the natural world through ceremony, craft, and magic. This is the way that I work with the kingdoms. You may well find that some things do not fit with your understanding or belief. Please feel free to change, adapt, and develop your own practices, which make sense to you. Nothing is carved in stone, including what is written here. The spirit of ceremony is very much "of the moment," unlike ritual which is the regular practice of a given procedure. Ceremony allows for interaction with each moment, but calls for a strong intuitive voice and perceptive listening skills.

Developing the heart is an excellent way to develop your magical gifts, because all this magical power is already present within yourself. It is just a question of finding the right keys to unlock your understanding. Be wise, be sensitive, and learn how to listen to everything around you with love and sincerity. All is then perfectly present for love to fill your life in many magical and mysterious ways. Enjoy!

INTRODUCTION

Magic exists! It originates from the Persian word **magia**, *meaning wisdom. Magic is a way of life that accepts the "mysterious," understands the language of all the kingdoms, and believes in the power of energy. Real magic, or High Magic, occurs when these signs are clearly understood and the four great gateways can then open up to you — those of love, light, wisdom, and truth. With these mighty gates opened we realize that there has never been a need to willfully command our future, or to manipulate events, because everything that happens in life has its own beauty.*

The key to all magic is love. With an open heart, many things can be learned and understood. **Love Magic** *will help you to connect to your own spiritual heart in simple yet effective ways. For example, it tells you about the herbs and flowers of love; it also explains how to make a massage oil for lovers; develop your relationship with the mineral kingdom; and divine with crystals. By working creatively with the love deities, you can also learn how to make your own magical equipment, such as a magic love mirror, staff, and wand. There are details of the ancient festivals dedicated to the goddess of love, together with suggestions on how to celebrate them as our ancestors once did. But, most important of all, you will be able to discover how to free your magical spirit so that every day becomes filled with natural wonder and delight. To honor the spirit of love and to honor the spirit of magic has been my aim, and to all those many friends who have helped me bring this about, I say "thank you." Om Shanti Om.*

GODDESSES AND GODS

Every civilization across time has had its own cultural representation of goddesses and gods. They are all aspects of the same energy. You will find that those I have chosen to work with can sometimes overlap each other, being one and the same deities but from different cultures across the world. Venus and Aphrodite are an example of this. The most well-known aspects of the love goddess have been included so that you can choose which one you feel most affinity with when weaving love magic.

The planet Venus has developed a rich culture of gods and goddesses associated with her varying levels of love and passion. These include the virgin – Brighid; the fertile woman – Aphrodite (the Greek goddess) and Venus (the Roman equivalent); the mother and provider – Demeter; and desirous or physical love – Eros/Cupid, Venus's son. Powerful representations of the winter or death aspect of the love goddess include Hathor and Circe.

BRIGHID

Brighid is a Northern European goddess of women, love, healing, agriculture, animal husbandry, and occult knowledge. She is honored during the spring months as a representation of the virgin bride. Her color is white, and her traditional ceremony calls for night processions to her sacred wells, bearing candles and bunches of snowdrops. The three-leaf clover, wells, the rowan tree, and shells are all sacred to her.

ABOVE *The rowan tree is a powerful psychic protector and is sacred to Brighid.*

RIGHT *Aphrodite was one of the great goddesses of Mount Olympus in Greek mythology.*

APHRODITE

Aphrodite is a Greek goddess who has the ability to bring lovers together. Her name means "of the sea," as she is believed to have been born of the foam of the ocean. There were many temples that were built in her honor in ancient Greece: she was an extremely popular goddess with lovers hoping for marriage. She can be especially called upon during the summer months, and in general love-working ceremonies for affection, partnership, and love. Burn frankincense and myrrh during her ceremonies. Make a window sticker (see page 917) with the Flower of Aphrodite to shine her influence into your home. The swan and dolphin are especially associated with her.

LEFT *Venus has strong links with the ocean; legend says that this was her birthplace.*

BELOW *Juno is a very old aspect of the moon and earth goddess.*

VENUS

Venus is the Roman equivalent to Aphrodite. She is patroness of vegetation and flowers, and represents the regenerative cycle of creation, as well as beauty, herbs, and physical love. She wears a lapis lazuli necklace, and is especially associated with the dove. Venus represents the independent woman, human love, and physical unions, as well as regeneration. She can be called upon for general love ceremonies, especially during the summer months. Burn pine essence (sacred to her lover) when working on difficult issues with a loved one, and incorporate roses (and any rose product) when working with her generally. The dove, roses, the ring, the ankh, the apple, rosemary, and copper are some of her sacred symbols.

JUNO LUCINA

Juno is a very ancient aspect of the goddess, and is the wife and sister of Jupiter. She represents the spirit of all women. She has many aspects, Lucina being "the light bearer." She is protector, mother, wife, sister, daughter, and grandmother. Her Greek equivalent is Hera. Her symbols include the lamp, the goose, the cuckoo, the peacock, the candle, the thunderbolt, the spear and shield, the fountain, the vulture, the lily, the fig tree, the pomegranate, and the stone malachite.

LEFT *Demeter is guardian of all women and an important magical goddess in Greek mythology.*

DEMETER

Demeter is a representation of the goddess as mother and provider. Patroness of grain and the harvest, she is associated with the planting of grain in the spring and with its harvesting in the fall. When we give thanks for all we have received from the earth in the fall, we are honoring this aspect of the goddess. Her sacred symbols include the fish, the dolphin, the white sow, the ant, the bee, loaves of bread, wheat, corn, all seeds, and sulfur.

FREYA

Freya is a Norse goddess associated with the number thirteen. She is goddess of love, marital union, and departed souls. In the cycle of human love there is a beginning, a middle, and an end; the freshness and newness of attraction, the consummation of passion, the fertile period, and then the physical parting, either because of an ending to the

relationship or because one soul departs the world. Freya is associated with the falcon, and rides in a cat-drawn chariot. Her symbols include furrows, May Day, the boar, the cat, the white horse, the hawk, raven and swan feathers, and amber.

ABOVE *The cats that pull Freya's chariot are called Bygul and Trjegul. Freya is protector of cats.*

ISHTAR

Ishtar is a Middle Eastern goddess of love and war, who is also associated with the moon and night-time. Known in Mesopotamia as "Mother of the fruitful breast," she will assist during severe relationship difficulties, and reveal the obstacles that hold love away from your life. Her symbols are the eight-pointed star, the pentagram, and the dove. She wears a rainbow necklace, and is also often represented by dragons, the serpent, and the sword. The sphere, veils, the palm leaf, and fig tree are all sacred to her.

LEFT Hathor is known as the mother of all gods and goddesses.

RIGHT Ishtar is also known as Innana and is the bringer of law and order.

HATHOR

Hathor, an Egyptian goddess of love, is guardian of all women, and is also the custodian of departed souls, caring for them when they have made their journey into the otherworld. Because of her associ-ation with death, she is primarily a Venusian winter goddess. She carries a sistrum (rattle) and uses it to protect souls from evil. She is also symbolized by dates and sycamore leaves, and is linked to the mandrake root (a powerful protective herb). Her sym-bols also include the goose, the golden egg, the lion and sphinx, and the long-horned cow. Her flower is the Egyptian lotus.

FLOWER OF APHRODITE WINDOW STICKER

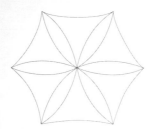

You will need:

a piece of thick paper

a square piece of clear acetate

masking tape

glass paints of your choice of colors

(to include pink and green)

outliner in copper-colored ink

Decide what size you would like the window sticker to be, and copy the design onto it. Make it approximately 3—5in (7.5—12cm) square, cut the paper to size. Place the acetate over the design and keep in place with masking tape at the edges. Using a water-soluble ink marker, trace the design onto the acetate. Work over the design with copper-colored glass outliner paint and leave it to dry. Fill in the spaces with your chosen colors. When completely dry, moisten the back of the acetate and fix to your window, saying as you do so, "Aphrodite queen of love, I set this sign to call my beloved here. Guide him / her well."

CIRCE

Circe represents the darker aspects of Venusian magic. She is patroness of physical love, sorcery, revenge, and dark magic, and is also known as "the spinner of fate." Circe, meaning circle, is the weaver of destinies, who can affect the lives of humans simply by knotting and braiding her hair. A powerful, no-nonsense representation of Venus, she is honored with offerings of honey and fruit, especially during the winter months. Beeswax candles can also be burned. The falcon and phenix are her symbolic representations.

EROS/CUPID

Cupid, the winged boy with a bow and arrow, is the Roman name and Eros is the Greek name for the same deity. The son of Venus/ Aphrodite, he is an aspect that represents erotic or lustful desire.

LOVE FESTIVALS

Love and fertility festivals were celebrated by our ancient ancestors. You can reawaken a connection to their powers through craft and ceremony. Every festival can be celebrated using the totems and symbols associated with each deity. There are no limits to the imagination when it comes to celebration of the ancient ways, as long as you keep to the appropriate deities for your particular task and keep your practices simple from the start.

RIGHT *A lover's keepsake box makes a romantic Valentine's gift.*

RIGHT *White candles and scallop shells are used to honor Brighid.*

FEBRUARY

February 2 is Brighid's Day, or Bride's Day, and represents the white goddess. It is the first love celebration in the yearly cycle: corn kernels, wheat grains, sea shells, and candles are used to celebrate the return of the goddess as bride and virgin (i.e. spring). Traditionally, Brighid was honored with candlelight processions to her holy shrines – especially wells. People would also strew reeds or sheaves of corn over the floor to make a place for her to sleep. They also repeated: "Brighid, Brighid, come into my house tonight," as they opened the doors of their houses to let her inside. You can honor Brighid with lighted white candles around a local well, or in a circle around a bowl of water in a garden, on the eve of February 1. Scallop shells, which are also sacred to Brighid, can be used as candleholders during this particular ceremony.

ABOVE *Light is important in all ceremonies to Juno Lucina (the light bearer).*

MARCH

In Roman culture March 1 was one of the festival days of Juno Lucina, the light bearer and goddess of women and marriage. It can be honored today by laying branches of oak on your altar and burning lilac essential oil in an oil burner; you may then ask for her guidance about a future marriage partner. You can meditate to the goddess on the evening of the last day of February, while burning grated fresh nutmeg on hot charcoal, first lighting four mauve candles in her honor. As you light each one say, "Juno Lucina — lady of the heart, I honor your presence, and I call upon you to guide me to the love I seek."

February 14 is Valentine's Day, and traditionally the greatest love festival of the year. In Roman times the festival was called Lupercalia and fell on February 14 and 15. It was held at Lupercal (the place where Romulus and Remus were suckled by a female of the wolf tribe) in honor of Juno Lucina, the light bearer, and was an opportunity for women to call to the nature deities for a child. It was later adopted as the Roman Saint's day to venerate acts of selfless love that he performed, during the time that people were killed for protecting the early Christians. Falling at the birth of the spring season, it is a time for giving gifts and tokens of love. Guidelines for making your own Valentine's keepsake box can be found on page 57.

APRIL–MAY

From the Latin word *Aprilis* (from to the verb "to open," as the flowers of the spring open), April is especially linked to the love goddess Aphrodite. It is the month of spring flowers and new growth. A three-day festival called the Floralia was held in Roman times between April 28 and May 3, dedicated to Flora (the Roman goddess of flowers) and Venus (the Roman goddess of love). During this time, posies in little baskets were secretly given as an act of love and blessing. May Day — a much more modern festival — is a continuation of this Roman celebration, giving thanks for new life and opportunity, with dancing around the maypole to weave ribbons around the symbolic staff of life.

JUNE

Probably derived from the name Junius, an aristocratic Roman family, June is considered a very fortunate month for weddings, and is associated with Juno. The summer solstice which falls on or around June 21 is an important time to connect with the spirit of love, fertility, and marriage. Honor the goddess at this time by making a magical staff (see pages 86–7).

In Babylonia the sacred days of Ishtar were June 1 and 2. Ishtar is the goddess of birth, life, and death, and is linked to the destiny of a failing relationship, but only when all else has not worked. She will help the hopeless situation, and so can be invoked at times when a relationship is going through difficulties. Her symbols include the dove, the pentagram, and the eight–pointed star. To call her, wait until just after a full moon, then find an alder, palm, or acacia tree (all three are sacred to her). Tie a red ribbon on one of her branches while thinking of the problem and say the following invocation: "Ishtar, queen of stars, all is not well with my lover and I. Send your spear to part the veil of illusion, which blinds us from the truth we need to learn. Thank you." Pull out a strand of your hair and lay it onto the branches as an offering of thanks.

RIGHT Seeds and grains can be used on magical crafts to the goddess, like on this staff.

JULY

July 19 in Egyptian times was the festival of Opet, which honored the sacred marriage of Isis and Osiris. It was also adopted by the Romans to celebrate the union of love between Venus and Adonis. It is therefore a good night to reaffirm your connection with a loved one, and to make a lovers' massage oil (see page 74).

AUGUST

Lammas, on August 1, is the first of three harvest festivals in the Celtic calendar. The Harvest festival honors Demeter, the goddess of love, as bountiful mother and faithful wife. Her presence can be seen in the fruits and crops displayed at the harvest festivals around the world. This is a festival of nourishment, of love as the giver, and so is an ideal opportunity to give some of your time to the needy. You may like to bake bread while thinking of Demeter and giving thanks for her gifts. Or you could lay sheaves of wheat and rye, or wheat grains and barley, on your altar during this festival; burn orange candles; and put a sprinkling of cassia bark on some burning charcoal to honor her.

ABOVE *Diwali is the New Year festival of the Hindus.*

OCTOBER

Diwali, the Festival of Lights, is sacred to Lakshmi, the Hindu goddess of happiness, love, and good fortune, and consort of Vishnu. The actual date of this festival is not fixed, although Diwali is usually celebrated during the month of October. At this festival, the sharing of love and joy between couples is celebrated and enjoyed with dancing and good food, as well as the lighting of numerous clay lamps. It is also a festival to Juno Lucina, the light bearer. You may like to light lamps and lanterns in your garden or home; have friends over for dinner; burn lotus oil; and, if you can obtain one, put a water lily or lotus into a bowl of water and place it on your altar in honor of the goddess of lights.

DECEMBER

The winter solstice falls on or around December 21 and marks the turning point from long dark nights to lengthening days. It is the time on the wheel of love when virgin goddesses gave birth to their children. It is symbolized by evergreens (holly, ivy, pine), mistletoe, red and white berries, frankincense, and myrrh. The last night of the year is traditionally "wishing night" in Mexico. To make a wish for a lover in the coming year go outside on a clear night and make a circle of evergreen branches, such as holly and ivy, and pine needles and cones. Place a bowl in the center and seven night lights around it. To a small amount of spring water, add seven drops of dragon's blood (red ink with *Calamus draco* added), three bay leaves, and three drops of lavender essential oil (to attract a male) or ylang-ylang (to attract a female). Stir the mixture with a cinnamon stick while making your wish. Make a small hole somewhere around the roots of an apple tree and pour in the fluid, or dig a small hole and pour the liquid over an organic apple before burying it. Say "thank you" to the apple or tree as you pour the fluid and fill in the hole.

RIGHT *Ivy is an evergreen and as such symbolizes eternal life.*

THE ANGEL OF LOVE

All of the kingdoms can be called upon when working magic. Everything is part of the Creator and as such will happily cooperate, especially where the call is genuine and sincere. Angels and archangels are servants of the Great Divinity, who is creator of all life. They do not always have wings; their wings are symbolic of their ascension in the world of spirit and symbolize their ability to travel interdimensionally to many realms across the universe. Their kingdom is one of service to Divine will, and they often act as messengers or helpers, rather like bridges from Heaven. Many people have reported seeing angels on battlefields, or have been guided out of danger by one. As children of God, humanity has a special place in the hearts of the angels and archangels, as they do in ours. Although they have not lived as human beings on Earth, they have a deep understanding of our frailties and needs.

ABOVE *Anael is honored with seven green candles.*

Anael is the angel of love. To honor Anael, it is important to be kind, loving, and gentle to all life. By right thought, action, and deed, you will ascend quickly to the realms of loving kindness, from where the secrets of the heart can be revealed. To aspire to angelic wisdom takes discipline and effort, but the rewards of opening to the angels means that love can flow to you from many different sources.

To honor Anael, lay seven green candles in a circle, with an emerald in the center in a bowl of water, on the Friday that falls just after a full moon. Light the candles and write on pieces of natural parchment seven things to work on that are holding you back in some way, such as greed, need, lust, jealousy, anger, hurt, and possessiveness. Then burn a piece of paper in each candle. Meditate upon releasing these things into the care of Anael, whom you can ask for guidance in the ways of peace and beauty. Sit in meditation for up to twenty minutes.

THE HEART OF ANAEL – A VISUALIZATION

You can ask a friend to read this to you as you journey, or you can tape it and play it back to yourself, allowing you to concentrate. The visualization will enable you to take a journey to your heart, assisted by a guide from the spirit world. This is very helpful in developing an understanding about who you really are. Center yourself for a few moments by breathing calmly, then close your eyes.

Imagine that you are in a sacred temple. There is a staircase leading up into the heavens, and standing beside it is a spirit helper. You begin to walk together up the stairway to the stars. This stairway goes up and up into the heavens, and as you ascend each stair, you feel lighter and lighter. Everything begins to sparkle like the stars. At the top of the stairs there is a copper door. You knock seven times, and the door opens. You and your guide go together through the doorway into the most beautiful room you have ever seen. In this room is an altar upon which sits a small sealed chest. You go over to the altar, and you see that there are seven candles burning and also a small key to open the chest. You open the lid and look inside. Look closely at what is inside, because this

is what lies deep in your heart. You note what is in the box, and may ask your guide questions in order to gain some understanding about what you have to do to aspire to the wisdom of your heart. Your guide seals the box again. You bid farewell to the heavenly room and return down the stairway to the sacred temple. Here your guide may wish to give you a gift – which you take if offered. With thanks and farewells you bring yourself fully present in your physical body again. Take some time to stretch, and as you breathe out, open your eyes.

ABOVE *The top of the stairway to the stars.*

VENUS
PLANET OF LOVE

The planet Venus is known magically as the planet of love. She rules the astrological signs of Libra and Taurus, although she will exert an influence upon every sign of the zodiac according to her placement in the birth chart. To find out where Venus is in your own chart, you will need to consult an astrologer. You can then refer to the details below to gain insights into how the Planet of Love influences your relationships.

RIGHT *The planet Venus is named after the Roman goddess of Love.*

VENUS IN ARIES

Passionate by nature, impulsive in love, Aries Venusians have a strong sexual drive, which they have to satisfy. They are loyal and lively friends, with lots of energy for creative projects. They have high physical energy.

VENUS IN TAURUS

Venus is exalted in Taurus, being its ruler. Taurus Venusians are loving, kind, generous, sensitive, and romantic. They have a strong tie to their family, which can lead to possessiveness. They are lovers of good food and company.

VENUS IN GEMINI

Gemini Venusians are good at communicating in relationships. They are not emotionally deep people, and this can lead to certain difficulties within personal relationships. They are fun friends and lively company.

VENUS IN CANCER

Cancerian Venusians are sensitive and kind, being in their element when they are needed. They can often feel insecure and be needy with a partner, which can be stifling in a relationship. They are sometimes moody when things do not go their way, but are gentle and caring.

VENUS IN LEO

The amorous Leo Venusian enjoys attention from admirers and colorful relationships. Loyal partners, creative by nature, Leo Venusians are drawn to the creative arts, living an opulent and interesting lifestyle. They need to guard against being too imposing in relationships. They are lovers of luxury.

VENUS IN VIRGO

It is important for Virgo Venusians to learn to be loving and kind in relationships and to guard against being overly critical with partners. Financial concerns in relationships will feature strongly with Virgo Venusians; they find it easier to be practical rather than emotional. They are responsible and genuine.

VENUS IN LIBRA

Libra, like Taurus, is ruled by the planet Venus and so is also exalted in Libra, which means that it increases the Venusian influence in the chart. Libra Venusians are romantic and affectionate, and are often idealistic about relationships. Libra Venusians need to feel loved and honored. They are kind and gentle.

VENUS IN SCORPIO

The Scorpio Venusians are usually enticing and alluring, having a magnetic effect upon others, drawing lovers into their lives. They are enigmatic and need to temper the intensity of sexual desires.

VENUS IN SAGITTARIUS

This placement means that, above all, Sagittarian Venusians need to feel free within any relationship, having an urge for excitement, stimulation, and an enthusiastic partner. They are fun-loving and interesting. This sign loves variety, is warm and friendly, and will most likely be highly individual.

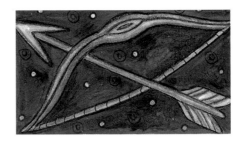

VENUS IN CAPRICORN

Venus in Capricorn is somewhat inhibited by the goat's need for practical characteristics, but it can lead to a tremendously loyal and faithful partner. Partnerships will normally have some kind of practical application, with any partner chosen carefully.

VENUS IN AQUARIUS

Aquarian Venusians have a tendency to be cool emotionally, sometimes even distant. They may find it hard to choose a partner, because they attract such interest with their magnetism. They seek the higher good for everyone they know.

VENUS IN PISCES

Here is the emotional placing of Venus, with Pisces Venusians being completely governed by what they feel. They are extremely romantic and will give up anything for love, often falling into the trap of being in love with love, just so that they can enjoy the feeling. They are kind and sympathetic.

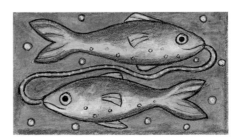

THE MESSENGERS OF LOVE

The universe is rich in the myriad ways that it speaks to us. This is revealed as we learn the language of the heart. To develop the heart, we must have genuine respect for all life, taking only what we need, with reverence and humility. Once the heart is open, sentient life will begin to speak in a different and beautifully simple way. For example, choose a flower that draws your eye and sit or stand close to it. Ask the deva (flower spirit) of the flower to come forward and commune with you – perhaps even help you with a problem that you have. Open yourself to be receptive, and wait patiently. The flower may need something from you too, so be prepared to give as well as receive!

❖

With practice, you will find messages coming to you from many places in nature. Say "thank you" for whatever you receive, and smile, because smiling is a great way of melting the heart into love.

FLOWER MESSENGERS

Each flower can have hundreds of meanings, depending upon who is asking the question. The flower meanings listed below should not be read as anything more than fun; the real truth is revealed by whatever you share with each spirit of the plant kingdom.

RIGHT *The buttercup gives out the message that "you are beautiful."*

RIGHT *A pink carnation means a meeting.*

Angelica – Your love inspires me

Buttercup – You are beautiful

Daffodil – Feelings are not reciprocated

Ivy tendrils – Marriage and constancy

Lavender – Friendship and respect

Love-lies-bleeding – You have broken my heart

Magnolia – Perseverance will bring better things

Mallow – I am devoted to you

Myrtle – I am drawn to you

Orange blossom – Pure love (a wedding flower)

Pink carnation – A woman's love

Pink rose – Pure and gentle love

Red carnation – A meeting will come soon

Red rose – I love you passionately

Rosemary – Remembering departed loved ones

Tulips – Our love is hopeless

Verbena – You are enchanting me

Veronica – You are my only love for now and always

Violet – My first sweet love

LEFT *Orange blossom means pure love.*

BELOW *Violets represent that first sweet love.*

ANIMAL MESSENGERS

Certain animals have associations with the goddesses of love. These include the bee, the dolphin and fishes, the dove, the sparrow, the swan, the bluebird, the white sow, the heron, the sheep, the goat, the peacock, and the lynx and other wild cats. The first day I began writing this book, a turtle dove visited the garden to wish me well. She came every day for a week, to give me something of her love for the book. I have not had a turtle dove in my garden before or since!

Birds have been used in auguries (predicting events) by our ancestors and can still be called upon today to help answer questions. Speak to the bird tribe by going to a wild place and, with a hand upon your heart, call to them to help you. Wait patiently and a bird (or even an animal) will connect with you. Watch, and listen to its message. Generally speaking, if a bird flies past to your left it means "no," and if it flies past to your right it means "yes." The birds listed here seem to like speaking to humans. Discover what they are saying to you personally by being quiet and listening.

Blackbird Listen to your soul; the inner voice
Dove Never forget that you are loved
Goose A move or change is imminent

Lone Crow Do not be afraid of spiritual change
One Magpie Be careful: something is not right
Two Magpies Joy is yours
An Owl (to your left) A change or loss
An Owl (to your right) Wisdom and understanding are the key
Pigeon A message
Robin The way will be shown to you; some sacrifice may be necessary
Skylark Celebrate your life with joyful voice
Sparrow Friendship and happiness come with simplicity, don't gossip
Starling Be discriminating; keep ideas and opinions to yourself at the moment
Woodpecker Keep focused upon your goal regardless of opposition, but be flexible
Wren You have the courage to survive in the big wide world

A bird coming into the house signifies a move for one of the residents soon. A black-colored bird knocking on glass is generally an omen. A large crow knocked on my conservatory door four times the night of Princess Diana's death. I knew immediately that something of great significance was about to occur.

RIGHT *The peacock is the sacred bird of Juno Lucina.*

THE DOVE

The dove has long associations with Aphrodite and Venus. A sexual symbol to followers of Aphrodite, she was a holy bird of peace and the holy spirit to Jews and later Christians.

THE SWAN

The swan is a bird sacred to the love goddess. It has the ability to carry the soul to the spirit world. In Saxon legend, Lohengrin was also known as the swan knight – protector of women.

THE WHITE SOW

The white sow, a female pig, is sacred to Demeter, and is an ancient symbol of the love goddess.

THE BEE

The bee (hymenoptra) is a sacred symbol of the goddess of love. Aphrodite was also known as Melissa (the queen bee), and Demeter was sometimes referred to as the great mother bee.

THE ANT

Ants are always busy and active, and as such are sacred symbols of the harvest goddess. Their activities below and above ground are seen to mirror their ability to move between the underworld and middle world (the physical plane) of earth.

THE DOLPHIN AND FISHES

The fish is an ancient symbol of the love goddess, as are the oceans and seawater, salt, and seashells. Fish are said to be an aphrodisiac. The dolphin derives its name from delphinos (womb). The dolphin represents Demeter in her sea goddess form and the snake represents her in her earth goddess form.

THE PEACOCK

Sacred to Juno, and to the goddess of wisdom, peacock feathers represent the eye of the goddess and her starry domain.

THE LYNX; WILD AND DOMESTIC CATS

Female cats represent the goddess as protector and magical familiar. The Egyptians had a deity called Bast – goddess of cats. She can still be called upon to find a lost animal or for protection from wild varieties!

LEFT *Bast is patroness of marriage, childbirth, and sex.*

TREES ASSOCIATED WITH LOVE

APPLE

Traditionally the apple refers to the crab apple, or wild apple. Cultivated varieties are still sacred to the goddess and both can be used in honor of love and lovers. Mistletoe grown on apple trees is the most sacred and potent variety for love magic, but be aware that the berries are poisonous. Harvest it carefully, and to keep its magical qualities, do not let it touch the ground.

FIG TREE

Juno Lucina — wife and sister of Jupiter — is honored with artifacts from the fig tree. It is believed that the fig was the original tree described in the Garden of Eden, which was later changed to be the apple tree.

ELDER

The elder tree, or witch tree, is a tree of Venus. It is considered very unlucky to tamper with an elder; one explanation is that it disturbs the witch that lives there. Highly venerated in the past by many peoples, the elder was considered a sacred tree of the earth mother, and to disturb her tree could cause her wrath, and bring death and bad luck to the person who disturbed her.

ABOVE *Figs are plump and fleshy, representing ripe fertility.*

DATE PALM

The palm tree is associated with Ishtar, the Babylonian goddess of love and war, and helper of hopeless situations in relationships: she will also reveal any obstacles in your love life. In ancient cultures the palm tree represented the phallus and was used in ceremonies that celebrated life and regeneration. Later, in the Christian Calendar, Palm Sunday became associated with palm-leaf crosses, but for different reasons. This occurred when Christ made his entrance into Jerusalem before his crucifixion. Alder and acacia are also sacred to Ishtar.

FRUIT TREES

The damson, cherry, fig, pomegranate, peach, and pear are all sacred trees of Venus, as well as the apple tree already mentioned. These fruits are ripe, plump, succulent, and juicy, and all (except the cherry which is considered virginal) were once used to represent the female genitalia in ceremonies to the love goddess. Any of these fruits can be given as an offering during your own love ceremonies to the goddess Venus.

SYCAMORE

The sycamore is the sacred tree of Hathor, the Egyptian goddess of love. Spirits of departed souls were said to dwell in the branches of this tree, as Hathor is guardian of departed souls. To show a lack of respect to this tree was, therefore, considered disrespectful of the ancestors. Coffins were made of sycamore wood, to ensure that Hathor would be close by to rekindle the breath of life and help the soul to its next incarnation. It is highly likely that the sycamore of Egyptian times was actually the fig tree.

Fruit pits have long been used for love divination. Take a random handful of cherries, eat the fruit, and then count the pits. Traditionally the rhyme goes, "Tinker, tailor, soldier, sailor, rich man, poor man, beggarman, thief." You could substitute your own modern professions to make the rhyme more appropriate to life today.

ABOVE *Place any fleshy fruit on your love altar when seeking prosperous or fertile relationships.*

ACTS OF LOVING KINDNESS

At another level there exists a divine spiritual love. Venus is servant to a greater will. Venusian gods and goddesses – as the immortal representations of human love – can take us only so far.

To rise higher, it is necessary to enter the temple of the heart to find devotion, compassion, loving kindness, and unconditional love. The greatest symbol of this love is the winged heart. Divine love rises not from working with the lesser gods and goddesses (who can assist with all the physical and emotional aspects of personal relationships), but from the one true god/goddess who is "father/mother to all things." Divine love is pure and unconditional. Many great teachers throughout history have spoken of the need to open the human heart with devotion and right practice. Love is not an external state that can be satisfied only by someone loving us; it first has to grow and flourish from within ourselves. Several times a day, perform simple selfless acts that are giving to others, including animals and plants. When you perform selfless acts, do not let anyone know that you are doing it; just quietly get on with it, do not seek praise. I call these, "acts of loving kindness," as my teacher did, when he showed me how to open my heart fully to others in this way.

A LOVING KINDNESS MEDITATION

For your loving kindness altar you will need:

a small bowl of water

a small bowl of earth

1 white candle

charcoal burner

(a heatproof incense container
for heating up charcoal blocks)

frankincense for burning

rose petals

a gold ink pen

a large bowl of water

a clear quartz crystal

First create a representation of the four elements of air, fire, water, and earth. Place the charcoal burner, with a piece of lit charcoal and frankincense grains in the east. Place the candle in the south and light it. Place the small bowl of water in the west, and the bowl of earth in the north. Write on the rose petals the name in gold ink of anyone who requires healing vibrations. This can also be done for victims of war, famine, or torture, by naming the place it is occurring if you know it, or by writing "suffering" instead. In the large bowl of water, place the quartz crystal and float the petals. Put the bowl in the center of your altar between the four elemental objects. Sit before your altar with your hands together in your lap and close your eyes. Center yourself for a few moments by breathing calmly and taking your focus down into yourself. When you feel calm, begin to meditate by saying to yourself on each inhalation "peace" and on each exhalation "all is well." When you feel balanced, open your hands to rest palms upward on each knee. Send loving energy to the crystal and from the crystal out to the person or people named in the bowl, or out into the world. Continue in this way for about twenty minutes. Keep your altar set up this way for at least twenty-four hours.

THE COLORS OF LOVE

Love is traditionally associated with pink and green, and these are the colors to use when working with love magic during the spring and summer. During the spring months, color your life with pink; during the summer with green; during the fall with ocher and orange; and during the winter with green and red together.

PINK – SPRING

Pink is a warm and pleasing color that lifts the spirits. Pink is a more gentle complement to green than red. It represents the dawning of love, purity of heart, spiritual love, and modesty. Pink and pale pastel flowers can be used when working magically with the love goddess in the springtime, as well as pink candles, and crystals such as rose quartz and strawberry quartz from Madagascar. Wear pink or pastel colors when performing love magic ceremonies during the spring; alternatively you may wear white.

GREEN – SUMMER

Green is the color of the heart chakra and is the color of Venus in her ripest aspect. It is also a powerful color in the natural world. Green is the balancing point between the seven colors of the rainbow, and can be used very effectively to harmonize any conflict, emotion, or confusion. Summer is the hottest time of the year, when fire and the color red are rulers. As the complementary color to red in the spectrum, green has a cooling and calming effect at this time of year, and reminds us that passion without love will burn itself out. Wear something green when working with love magic in the summer.

RED/GREEN – WINTER

Red is the color of passion, life, and vitality. The traditional colors of the winter season are red and green, red being used with evergreens to symbolize everlasting life and the renewal of warmth and light upon the earth. On the wheel of the year it is the time of quiet reflection and rest, when energy is gathered before another period of growth begins in the spring. Red represents the blood of life and the female menses, as well as passionate union. A primary color, red is associated with the base chakra, the chakra of survival and security. Use red to encourage strength and power in magical ceremonies, or to ward off negativity.

OCHER/ORANGE – FALL

When the Venusian wheel – the circle of the love goddess as she turns through the seasons – turns back to the earth and harvest time, the love goddess is represented as the mother, nurturer, and provider. Orange is the color associated with the reproductive chakra in the body, and symbolizes regeneration. It is also a color filled with energy and promise. It is therefore a suitable color to honor the fall season on the wheel of love, because we are not only wanting to give thanks for the harvest, but also hoping for her blessings in the year to come.

MARCH
TO MAY

A SPRING ALTAR

East is the direction of beings and creatures of the
air, so display feathers from birds that are associated with love
(see pages 30–1). Take only feathers that present themselves to you:
never raid nesting sites or disturb birds that are sitting on eggs. To do so
would "anger" the goddess and render your magical tool ineffective, because the
energy with which it was obtained was not pure in heart. If I ask with my hand on my
heart for a feather to place on my love altar, I find that one will always appear if it is
necessary – and always with perfect timing.

The spring flowers that come under the influence of Venus include primroses, pansies
and violets, tulips, apple blossom, periwinkle, hyacinth, bluebell, lilac, and forget-me-nots.
You can offer some flowering spring bulbs growing in pots, hyacinths for example, and
then plant them outside to bloom another season, once spring has passed. The
color of the spring season when dedicated to love is pink. Use a pair of pink
candles, and two rose quartz or strawberry quartz crystals, when laying
out your design.

PSYCHIC SPRING CLEANING

Spring is the beginning of a new cycle and so is a good time to fully cleanse, purify, and sanctify your altar room or area before dedicating it to the rising powers of the East. The East comes into influence in the spring. You can also cleanse yourself by smudging with a cleansing herb such as mountain sage, juniper, or cypress. This is a simple yet effective way to keep yourself psychically pure. Take a small handful of the chosen herb and put it into a heatproof container. Seashells are excellent for this, but be aware that smudge bowls can get very hot, so do not place them directly on surfaces or carpets. Light the herb and fan the smoke around your body, under your feet and arms, over your head, and around your back. A feather can be used to move the smoke. Breathe in a little of the smoke and visualize it cleansing your inner world as well. Pass the feather through the smoke to close the cleansing ceremony.

For springtime ceremonies and magic, face east. The most potent time for spell-weaving is during the crescent to first quarter phase of the moon.

Not only is it necessary to clean away physical matter from your magical area, but psychic energy that may be building up there also needs to be dealt with. First physically clean the room, and then, using birch twigs tied together with jute or twine, or a birch broom, start in the top right-hand corner of the area, and sweep toward the middle of the room, saying as you do so, "Broom clear, broom clean matter from the world unseen. You, with winter must depart, to make way for the virgin's heart."

Continue clockwise around the room sweeping into the middle of it as you go.

Once the circle of sweeping is completed, gather your "psychic" matter into a dustpan and put it into a paper bag. Burn this bag or bury it beneath a yew, cedar, or cypress tree.

ABOVE *The birch broom has been used for centuries to sweep out the old and cleanse the environment from psychic and physical debris.*

A SPRING LOVE SPELL

Spring is the time, on the wheel of love, for new beginnings. This spell calls for a new beginning in your love life, and you will need to face east when casting it. The best time to do it is during the very new moon, when it is still a crescent. First cleanse your body, then dress in white or pastel-colored clothes. Burn some rose essential oil in an aromatherapy burner.

You will need:

a bowl of natural sea salt

rose incense

1 red candle

a small bowl of water

a small bowl of earth

2 pink candles

2 pink paper hearts

a parchment pen

dragon's blood ink (see page 21)

a 7–in/17.5cm length of

thin pink ribbon to bind

1 rose quartz crystal

Place the ingredients in the middle of the room where you have chosen to weave this spell. Moving clockwise, sprinkle natural sea salt in a large circle around yourself, making sure that the beginning and the end join together. Pick up the incense and hold up either your lover's wand (see page 51) or your index and middle fingers of your dominant hand, and begin to cast a circle around yourself. As you do this say, "Hail to the guardians and beings of the East! I honor your powers and call for your presence." Put down the incense. Turn to the south and say, "Hail to the guardians and beings of the South! I honor your powers and call for your presence." Put down and light the red candle.

Pick up the bowl of water. Turn west and say, "Hail to the guardians and beings of the West! I honor your powers and call for your presence." Put down the water. Pick up the bowl of earth. Turn to the north and say, "Hail to the guardians and beings of the North! I honor your powers and call for your presence." Put down the earth. Now say, "The circle is cast – let the magic begin."

Put the two pink candles in front of you and light them, saying, "Hail to thee holy mother of hearts! I light these lights to honor your sacred presence. Please come and hear me." Take one paper heart and write in dragon's blood ink the words, "My loving heart." Write on the other heart: "My lover's heart." Place them face together and bind gently with the pink ribbon, saying seven times as you do so, "Our hearts are united as one, so may we lovers be drawn together." Place this bundle in the center of your altar.

Sit before the altar for up to twenty minutes with your palms facing upward, while visualizing yourself being filled with love. Send your love out to a lover and call her/him to you. (Remember not to name or think of anyone in particular during this time, lest you manipulate them by mistake or interfere with their own free will.)

Move counterclockwise, starting with the candle in the north, and say, "Hail and farewell to the guardians and beings of the North! Thank you for your presence." Continue in this way until all the candles have been extinguished. Make a cut in the circle of salt, while saying, "This spell is done."

Keep the bundle of hearts on the center of your altar with a rose quartz crystal placed on top, until your lover arrives. When he/she comes, ceremoniously bury or burn it, giving thanks.

The daisy is a flower of Venus, which is the reason for the following tradition. State very clearly that you wish to know if a particular person has romantic feelings toward you. Then scan the ground carefully to see which daisy is calling you. Finally, pull off the petals one by one, saying "yes" and "no." The final petal will reveal a positive or negative answer.

SPRING FLOWERS OF LOVE

PRIMROSE (*PRIMULA VULGARIS*)

The primrose is the sacred flower of Freya, one of the goddesses of Venus. It grows in most of Europe in hedgerows, meadows, and woodland, where their familiar pale yellow flowers can be recognized. When collecting primroses, choose a place where they are abundant and pick only a few.

PANSY (*VIOLA TRICOLOR*)

Traditionally, the pansy is also known as Heartsease, because of its intimate link with the heart. It is worn to attract love, and can be included in love posies to let your lover know of your attraction!

CYCLAMEN
(*CYCLAMEN EUROPAEUM*)

Cyclamen is a flower of Venus as well as Hecate (the goddess of the dark moon), and represents protection from grief, as well as love. Cyclamen can also be placed in a bedroom to ensure healthy sleep. It can help someone deal with grief, too.

WILD VIOLETS (*VIOLA ODORATA*)

Violets are well known as flowers of the love goddess. Parma violet sweets used to be used to sweeten the breath, and the aroma of violets is said to be an aphrodisiac. Their tiny delicate flowers are perfectly formed, hinting at another of the violet's attributes – modesty.

APPLE BLOSSOM (*PYRUS MALUS*)

Apple blossom comes into flower on the fruit trees in early May. It is the bloom most associated with the goddess of love. Known as the Silver Bough in the Celtic tradition, the crab apple (and its cultivated varieties) is endowed with magical qualities that can link you to the world of spirit.

FORGET–ME–NOT (*MYOSOTIS SYMPHYTIPHOLIA*)

In German tradition, these delicate blue flowers are associated with love. An amorous knight fell into a river and drowned while trying to pick some for his beloved – hence the title. They represent remembrance of love when there is a forced parting.

FRAGRANCE OF LOVE

This spring love spritzer can help to revitalize the spirits of the heart and home, and bring blessings of love, happiness, and joy.

SPRING LOVE SPRITZER

Use this spritzer primarily as a room spray to help draw love into your home or work environment. It can be used as a body spritzer occasionally, by misting it around your aura when your spirits are low, to bring back a feeling of joy and optimism. However, be aware that prolonged personal use of any product has the potential to cause irritation to the skin. Although completely safe for cosmetic use, it should not form part of a daily routine for longer than two weeks at a time.

Before starting, bless and potentize your ingredients to awaken their magical qualities (see page 41). Take one of the ingredients (or the utensils), e.g. distilled water, and pass it through the incense smoke, saying, "By the powers of the East wind, this distilled water is cleansed and purified." Move south and say as you pass it through the candle flame, "By the powers of the South wind, this distilled water is now cleansed and purified." Turn west and say as you sprinkle some water upon the bottle, "By the powers of the West wind, this distilled water is now

You will need:

frankincense crystals or incense

a red candle

a small bowl of spring water

a small bowl of earth

distilled water

1 tsp vodka

hyacinth or lilac flowers

marjoram essential oil

geranium essential oil

crab apple essence (Bach Flower Remedy)

red rosebud essence (Harebell Remedies)

a Kilner jar

a spray bottle

purified," and do the same for the north. Lay your object down on the center of the altar between the four offerings. Cleanse all the ingredients thus.

Sit in front of your altar, and call to Venus: open your hands, palm upward, and say, "Our Lady Aphrodite, goddess of flowering love, I call to you to bring your blessings to this fragrance of love – and so awaken the magical heart that dwells within. Thank you." The ingredients are now ready.

Place a circle of clean and unbruised blooms around a Kilner jar containing 3½ fl oz (100 ml) of distilled water, and one teaspoonful of vodka, as an offering to call in the goddess of love. Stir for several minutes while thinking of love and vitality. Add 6–8 drops each of marjoram oil, geranium oil, and crab apple and red rosebud essence. Seal the lid to allow the concoction to infuse with the water, and shake the bottle regularly over the next twenty-four hours. Decant the scented water into the spritzer container, discarding all the organic matter. Keep in a cool, dry place.

MARJORAM

Marjoram brings confidence and the ability to nurture oneself. It is reassuring and comforting to the emotions.

GERANIUM

Geranium helps to bring love and joy, and contact with the emotions. It encourages harmony and good humor between male and female.

CRAB APPLE

Crab apple flower essence is a general cleanser and tonic, and is ideal for helping to release the old to make way for the new. It also prepares for the new season of spring with its new growth and promise.

RED ROSEBUD

Red rosebud opens us up to loving feelings in a light-hearted and gentle way, while ensuring that we feel safe in this expansive process.

LEFT *You can spritz your aura or your environment with this fragrance of love.*

A SPRING LOVE POTION

Spring is an ideal time for cleansing, as we know. This love potion recipe will help to prepare you for love and loving vibrations by cleansing the old, thus making way for new opportunities.

Vibrational essences have been used by peoples all over the world for thousands of years, and flower and crystal essences have become increasingly popular due to the pioneering work of Dr. Edward Bach during the 1930s. Since his rediscovery of the power of vibrational essences for healing and spiritual growth, many people across the world are now producing a wide range of transformational remedies.

This love potion utilizes the same principles as a vibrational essence, and so should not be stored near to electrical equipment, in a refrigerator, or in direct heat or sunlight. Store your love potion in a cool, dry cupboard when not in use. It is best to make this potion during the crescent (new) moon phase.

You will need:

apple or cherry blossoms
8 cloves
7 small tumbled rose quartz crystals
a small glass bowl
spring water
1 teaspoon natural undyed sea salt
2 pink candles
7 primrose flowerheads
a miniature bottle of vodka
dropper bottle

Decorate your altar with two vases of spring blossoms such as apple or cherry. Lay the cloves in the east, south, west, and north, and then in the northeast, southeast, southwest, and northwest, to make a circle. Take three crystals and place one in the north, one in the southeast, and one in the southwest. Take another three crystals and place one in the south, one in the northeast, and one in the northwest, to form two interlocking triangles, or a six-pointed star. This star is the ancient Sanskrit symbol for the heart chakra and so is potent for love magic, as well as incorporating the number six – which is sacred to Aphrodite.

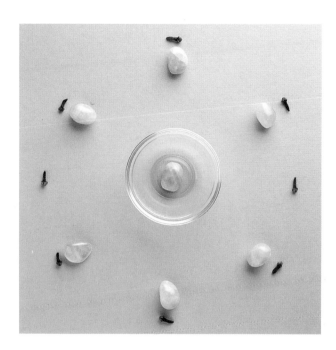

LEFT *Cloves act as attractors, empowering the rose quartz crystals to activate loving vibrations in the love potion.*

Purify the glass bowl by swirling around it some spring water containing the salt, and rinse. Place the two pink candles on either side of the circle of cloves and light them. Set the now empty glass bowl in the center of the star, and place the seventh rose quartz inside. Cover the crystal with spring water. Take each primrose flowerhead in turn and say anything that you are positively seeking (e.g. companionship, laughter, sharing, or joy – it must be a positive remark) as you place it onto the surface of the water. With your hands placed palms upward on your lap say: "Great Mother as maiden of the spring, this potion I make within the ring. Circles of energy gather above to empower this potion with the spirit of love."

Sit in meditation for about twenty minutes while the potion is empowered by the helpful spirits. Say "thank you" to those who have empowered your potion, then blow out the candles and leave the potion undisturbed for three hours. Pour vodka into the dropper bottle until one-third full, and top up the bottle with the potion.

Take seven drops of the potion in a glass of spring water morning and evening for one month, thinking of pure love as you do so. Store in a cool, dry place, and discard after one month.

SPRING CRAFTS

The magical wand is an ancient magical tool associated
with the divine feminine. It represents transformation and is sometimes referred to as a witches' wand. You can make several wands and
dedicate them to various deities and uses. Each wand is usually tipped with a
crystal, and decorated in a fashion that reflects the uses of the wand. A healing
wand might be made of willow, have a turquoise crystal at its tip, and be decorated
with blue and silver ribbons, wound with silver wire, and dedicated to the moon.

The lover's wand shown here has been made of apple wood, a tree sacred to the love
goddess. You will need to gather your own piece of wood for your wand in a sacred way.
Rachel, the maker of the wand, remembered an apple orchard owned by "good" people
and they allowed her to go there. She wandered around the old trees in the orchard
until she spotted a young and slender branch, which the tree said was her wand.
Holding the spirit of love and connectedness throughout, she began to
gather objects and place them upon her altar until it was time for her
to use them.

A LOVER'S WAND

You will need:

a piece of apple, pear, damson, elder, or magnolia wood

coarse and fine sandpaper

beeswax polish

glue

a rose quartz crystal

pink and green ribbons

copper wire

decorative love charms

On a new moon day (between the first and fourth day of the appearance of the crescent) go to your chosen site and ask with sincerity to be guided to your lover's wand: the local spirits in that place will tell you were to go.

Once you have found the place where your wand will come from, choose the piece of wood that seems right for you, ask respectfully to take it, and give thanks by leaving a small crystal, strand of hair, or other small object that will not harm local wildlife.

Strip the bark if you like and smoothe the wood with the coarse then the fine sandpaper. Polish it with beeswax. The wand is now ready for cleansing (see page 46, making a Love Spritzer). Once this has been completed, dedicate and bless your wand:

"Aphrodite, queen of heaven and earth, fill this wand with the spirit of love, that it may be used for love and in the service of the heart. I ask your blessings upon it: may it now be filled with all that is hallowed to life, for the highest good of all."

Glue the crystal to the tip of the wand. Wrap the ribbons around the stem, and interlace them with the copper wire wherever you feel drawn to put it. Then decorate the wand with your charms, hanging them from ribbons or threads, or gluing them in place – whichever you feel is most appropriate.

How you make this wand will make it personal and magical to you, so let your inspiration flow and be guided by the spirit of love. The wand can be used to cast circles of love and to direct loving energy. Keep the wand beneath your altar, wrapped in green silk cloth when not in use.

A LOVE TALISMAN

A talisman is an object that has been charged and specifically programed with magical powers. This talisman is a love talisman to the spirit of Venus and all her specific attributes – of love, joy, beauty, creativity, and fertility. Writing the sigil (pattern) of your name upon the Venusian magic square and then affirming your wish will potentize the words.

Creating a talisman offers an ideal opportunity to gather the symbols of love and place them on your altar. These could be heart trinkets, swan feathers, fig leaves, apple blossom, pink candles, and other items you have around according to the season and the time of year.

For the basic altar you will need:

rose incense or essential oil and aromatherapy burner
1 red candle
a small bowl of water
a small bowl of earth
2 pink candles
love charms (optional, but lovely to include)
natural paper, 3½in x 3½in / 9cm x 9cm
dragon's blood ink (see page 21)
a handful of cloves
green silk pouch

First create a representation of the four elements of air, fire, water, and earth. Place the burning bowl of incense in the east; the red candle in the south, then light it; the bowl of water in the west; and the bowl of earth in the north, invoking the four directions as you do so. Place the two pink candles in the center, and love charms wherever you choose. Light the burner and candles.

Working near to your altar, begin by translating the name you are best known by into a pattern, by changing the letters of your name into numbers.

1	2	3	4	5	6	7	8	9
A	B	C	D	E	F	G	H	I
J	K	L	M	N	O	P	Q	R
S	T	U	V	W	X	Y	Z	

For example, Steve becomes 12545.

Draw out the talisman of Venus onto a piece of
paper as below and practice drawing the pattern of
your name onto it.

22	47	16	41	10	35	4
5	23	48	17	42	11	29
30	6	24	49	81	36	12
13	31	7	25	43	19	37
38	14	32	1	26	44	20
21	39	8	33	2	27	45
46	15	40	9	34	3	28

The sigil of Steve on the talisman of Venus will
look like this:

22	47	16	41	10	35	4
5	23	48	17	42	11	29
30	6	24	49	81	36	12
13	31	7	25	43	19	37
38	14	32	1	26	44	20
21	39	8	33	2	27	45
46	15	40	9	34	3	28

Once you are confident that you have mastered
your sigil, write on your plain piece of paper (do not
add the numbers), and use dragon's blood ink to
draw the sigil of your name in the top right-hand

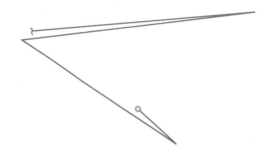

corner of the paper. In the remaining space write,
"Whoever has chosen to fill my heart with joy, come
and heed my call for love." Copy this seal onto the
other side of the paper.

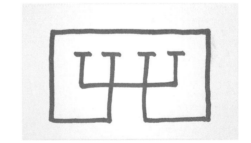

This is the seal of the Angel of Venus, and acts like
a calling card to her, activating her energy and
cooperation. It is best that this planetary seal is
hand- drawn by yourself on a piece of handmade
paper. Remember to conduct this ceremony mind-
fully and take this interaction with Venus seriously.
You must always be aware of what you are doing.

A SPRING LOVE POSY

Spring holds hope and promise and is the time when new life emerges from the earth. On the wheel of love it represents a heart full of potential. As part of ancient celebrations to the union of the god and goddess, May Day was celebrated with pairing in the woods and fields, as well as dancing around a maypole decked with colored ribbons.

Lovers and loved ones could be surprised to find an anonymous gift of a small basket of spring flowers on their doorstep on May Day morning. This activity is particularly nice to share with children.

It is important to remember that some flowers are endangered and it is illegal to remove them from where they are growing. Be careful how much you take from any one spot and do not disturb rare or endangered species.

You will need:

a small basket of woven wood

floristry foam

floristry wires

spring flowers and greenery, such as ivy

Cut the floristry foam to fit the basket, then soak it well in water. Meanwhile, attach floristry wires to the flower stems. Insert the foam into the basket and begin pressing in the wired flowers, filling up the basket with your arrangement. Place the larger flowers in the central area and the smaller flowers toward the edge. Add greenery and ivy leaves to fill the gaps and break up the color. Attach ribbons to the handle of the basket if you wish.

You will need:

mosquito netting or window screening

an old picture frame

staple gun

assorted white and pink tissue paper, torn into strips

paper towels, and other soft thick paper,

torn into small pieces

a blender

water

a large bowl

absorbent cloths

small sequins

dried rose petals, lavender, honeysuckle,

bush geranium, and marigold leaves

blotting paper

rolling pin

sheet of glass

dried rosebuds

box frame

white (PVA) glue

Cut the netting to the size of the frame and staple it in place. Put the torn-up pieces of paper into the blender. Cover with water and leave to soak for a few minutes. Then blend to produce a fine watery pulp, adding more water if necessary. Pour the pulp into the bowl. Continue soaking and blending the papers until there is a deep layer of pulp in the bowl.

Dip the netting underneath the pulp to form a layer on the screen about 1 in/2.5 cm thick. Move the netting about so that the pulp settles evenly on the surface. Allow the excess water to drain away.

While the paper pulp is still wet, form the pulp into a heart shape. Then you can begin to press it dry with absorbent cloths, but don't make it completely dry. While it is still damp, press your chosen petals, sequins, seeds, grasses and leaves, working them into the surface of the paper to secure them firmly in place. You can also use good quality fresh flowers to decorate your heart.

Turn the paper heart out onto newspaper. Place a sheet of blotting paper over it and use a rolling pin to press out as much water as possible. You may have to make one or two attempts before you get the correct consistency of pulp. Transfer the heart shape onto some glass and leave it in a warm place to dry completely.

When it is dry, glue rose buds and other petals onto the surface. Place the heart into the box frame and glue in place. Surround it with mementos or leave it for the recipient to fill.

Rachael added a key to her keepsake box, and laid a verse photocopied on acetate across the frame so that the heart is seen through the words:

"Thank you for teaching me that love is an art and for reaching the closed places locked in my heart."

SPRING LOVE RECIPES

Spring is traditionally associated with the regeneration
of life, as flowers and shoots appear above the ground. The egg is
often used in magic to symbolize the creative potential of the feminine.
Several myths suggest that the egg is the origin of life, including some from
India, China, and Greece. The ancient Egyptians believed that their sun god Ra was
hatched from a cosmic egg laid by the Nile Goose. Geese are sacred to Juno, signifying
love, protection, and the "good woman," the goose being considered the carer of the sun
during the winter until he rises in power the following year.

❖

As with all magical workings, it is best to use ingredients that are as natural as possible. Try
to obtain organic products – use non-organic ingredients when organic is not available.
Shaped tins can be hired from most reputable baker's shops – heart shapes bring a
romantic touch to the finished cake. The egg is seen as the womb that contains the
origin of life, so when breaking them into the mixture, visualize that you are
creating a cake for the sacred heart and give thanks to creation for the
powers of your own "cosmic" eggs.

PASSION CAKE

For the cake mixture you will need:

4 oz / 100 g light soft brown sugar

2 eggs

8 oz / 200 g self-rising flour (80% whole-wheat is best)

2 oz / 50 g organic walnuts (chopped)

4 oz / 100 g grated carrots

2 mashed bananas

2 tsp baking powder

Combine the sugar and eggs in a mixing bowl with a wooden spoon, then add all the other ingredients. Stir well while thinking of love surrounding you (and your loved ones, if appropriate) and blessing your life in the year ahead. Transfer the mixture to a greased, lined loaf tin (or shaped tin). Place it in the

middle of a medium hot oven (350°F/180°C/Gas Mark 4) for about one hour, until the cake is golden brown. Turn out and leave to cool on a wire rack.

For the icing you will need:

7oz / 175g full fat cream cheese

4oz / 100g icing sugar

2oz / 50g butter

the grated rind of an orange

Mix the cream cheese with a wooden spoon until soft and thoroughly blended. Add the icing sugar, butter, and orange rind to the icing, and stir well. Cover the cake completely with the icing mixture.

For the crystallized primroses you will need:

1 egg white

5 perfect primrose flower heads

caster sugar

Whisk the egg white in a clean, dry bowl until it is fluffy. Dip the flowerheads into the mixture, then sprinkle the sugar to completely cover them. Leave them to dry and harden. Decorate the top of the cake with these flowers. (In the recipe shown, strands of orange peel were used instead.)

SPRING LOVE COCKTAIL

Before making violet tea, first take a gift for the flower devas to a place where violets (or other wild flowers) are growing, as an offering for their assistance in empowering your collection of flowers and leaves. The gift could be a small crystal of Venus, an apple cut crosswise so that the five pointed seed pods are visible, or something sweet (which the elementals love!) Before you start collecting, lay down your offering and say:

"Spirits of the wild wood, I come in peace, to ask your assistance and empowerment of this magical flower of love. I ask permission to take some to make a love cocktail, so that my heart may sing with joy. Please accept my gift in return."

Wait a few moments and make sure that the devas agree to your request before gently collecting a handful of the heart-shaped leaves and a small handful of the flowers.

If you have to purchase violets from a florist, take them outside to a park or garden, and discreetly explain to the local flowers that you have come to ask the devas for their blessing. Lay your purchased violets on the ground. Make your request and offering as outlined above.

You will need:

a handful of violet leaves

a small handful of violet flowers

a ceramic pestle and mortar (do not use any metal utensils or containers)

boiling spring water

Cheesecloth (muslin) strainer

honey or natural sugar, such as agave (cactus) or brown rice syrup, to sweeten

LEFT *Violets have long associations with clearing a headache.*

BELOW *Violet flowers can bring good luck when carried.*

Using the pestle and mortar, crush and bruise the flowers and leaves. Put the compound into a ceramic cup and cover with boiling spring water. Stir in a clockwise direction for one minute and then leave to infuse and cool for five minutes. Strain and serve, while daydreaming of meeting a lover or thinking nice thoughts of a loved one.

Violets are sacred to Aphrodite, the Greek goddess of love. There are over 100 varieties found in temperate climates across the world. Wild violets have heart-shaped leaves and dark purple flowers. Variations of the purple color include pale lilac, white, and pale pink flowers, and are often found growing close together.

Found in shaded woodlands, waysides, and hedgerows, violets are rarely seen in urban areas, because they have delicate leaves that are sensitive to smoke and pollution. Their small flowers bloom between February and April and are rich in nectar,

which would attract bees, though it is a little early in the season for them.

Medicinally, syrup of violets has been used for coughs, colds, bronchitis, and other respiratory problems. It is therefore an ideal ingredient for a tonic in spring when bronchial complaints tend to be commonplace. An infusion of violets is also helpful in alleviating headaches. When out walking, pick a few leaves (honoring the devas with a strand of your hair in return, of course!) and rub them on your temples to clear a muggy head.

JUNE
TO AUGUST

A SUMMER ALTAR

On the wheel of love, summer is the power time for
the masculine energies of passion, virility, and strength. Both
male and females are at their most productive. Venus is queen at this
time of year, fertile and ripening as she comes into womanhood. Approaching
the summer solstice is the time for fulfillment magic, to call for the manifestation
of something positive. Your summer altar should honor the abundance and richness
of life at this time of year with the color of Mother Nature – green. Lay a green altar
cloth, green candles, dove feathers, lapis lazuli, peridot, jade items and any other emerald
green stones; and, of course, roses for your general summer altar.

Face south during summer ceremonies and meditations. The potent time for love magic
is between the first quarter of the moon and the days leading up to and the actual
night of the full moon. Flowers of the summer love goddess include the daisy,
magnolia, rose, spearmint, sweet pea, thyme, tansy, passionflower, geranium, iris,
camomile, pink geranium, foxglove, orchid, wild (or dog) rose, elderflower,
hibiscus, mugwort, myrtle, vervain, and yarrow.

WALKABOUT

The abundance of summer makes it a good time of year to go on a "walkabout" (walking the sacred Aboriginal way) to gather objects and items for your summer altar. On a walkabout you allow yourself to be guided by the goddess of love, following signs and feelings, with no particular destination in mind.

The goddess could appear as a butterfly or dragonfly, a dove or pigeon call, the rustling of leaves in an elder tree – whatever catches your attention on your walkabout should be noted and then followed.

Begin your journey by sitting in front of your altar (covered with a green cloth with two green candles burning). Open your heart and come to a place of stillness within. When you feel silent and calm say:

"Lady Venus; Queen of nature, this request I make: guide me to your gifts of love on the journey I now take, into your wild and greenest places. Help me find my way, Lady Venus, I shall follow where you lead today."

Sit in silent meditation, making your connection with the goddess. When you feel connected to her, feel which direction you would like to take, and from where you would like to begin your journey (it may involve a car journey). Once at your starting point, tell your surroundings why you are there and that you are seeking items for your summer love altar. A walkabout has no set plan, and it is important to keep a very open mind about what you may find. Try not to "look," but instead wander with purpose, so that each small thing can be recognized. Remember, too, that not everything you find will be for your use. Make sure before you take anything that it feels right to remove it. Objects that you may find include feathers, stones, leaves, fruit and seed pods, animal bones, and flowers. Birdsong may lead you upon a magical journey through the woods and the song itself may be the message, so do not feel disheartened if "nothing" seems to appear. You are never alone on a walkabout. Sometimes this kind of simplicity is all you need to bring back to your altar, and it will be carried in your heart.

A SUMMER SPELL

LEFT *Any pipes can be used in magic, once blessed and consecrated for ceremony.*

Summer is a wonderful time of year to perform magic outside, especially at dawn or dusk. This summer love spell is called "Wheel of Love." The thirteen stones that are required for this ceremony should be of a reasonable size so that they are easy to transport to your chosen site.

You will need:

a gift for the nature spirits (crystal, posy, craft)

thirteen stones

a small pipe, tobacco, and matches

a sage smudging stick or sage leaves

ABOVE *Choose each stone with awareness in this ceremony.*

Begin by honoring the spirits of your chosen place for this spell by offering your gift. Bless and welcome each stone. Mentally draw a circle on the ground and choose four stones. Facing south, hold the first stone to your heart and call for the assistance and protection of the powers of the south wind. Then place it on the ground at the southern point of the circle. Similarly, invoke and place the other three stones in turn for north, west, and east.

Take your fifth stone and hold it up to the heavens saying, "Grandfather Sky, I call for your clear sight and ask you to help me here today. Thank you." Then lay aside this sky stone.

Take your sixth stone and touch the earth with it, saying, "Grandmother Earth, I give thanks to you for supporting and nurturing me throughout my life and ask you to bring your magical powers to this circle of love today." Then lay this earth stone aside too.

Take your seventh stone and hold it to your heart, calling upon the Creator of all Things to bring a blessing upon your ceremony and to guide you in the ways of love, light, wisdom, and truth. Lay down this Creator stone separately from the others.

Use the remaining six stones to make a spiral into the center of the circle, adding the sky and earth stone last. Place the Creator stone in the center and on this place the pipe and tobacco.

Light the smudge and use the smoke to cleanse yourself and the circle, allowing the smoke to fill the area. Move clockwise toward the center and then pass the smoke over the pipe and tobacco. Pick up the pipe and hold it to your heart for a short while. Holding it in your right hand, take a small pinch of tobacco for each direction, another for all life, one for Grandmother Earth, one for Grandfather Sky, and one for the Great Mystery. Finally, take small pinches of tobacco for each wish that you have, until the pipe is full. Facing toward the center of the spiral, light the pipe and smoke it (you do not have to inhale the smoke), allowing the trails to float into the heavens. Visualize your wishes being carried to the Creator to be heard. Smoke the pipe until the tobacco is completely burned. This ceremony can be performed for your own wishes or for the benefit of any sentient life, by filling the pipe with appropriate prayers. Close your ceremony by removing the stones in reverse order, saying your thanks as you do so.

THE FRUITS OF LOVE

All the ripe, succulent, and juicy fruits are associated with Venus. These include the strawberry, banana, fig, watermelon, peach, avocado, date, blackberry, apple, damson, cherry, and grape.

STRAWBERRY

Strawberries have a very high iron content and so are excellent for improving the blood. They have been used for centuries as a skin conditioner, having the ability to reduce wrinkles and lines on the face and to cleanse the complexion generally. To make a cleansing face mask from strawberries, gather a handful of wild strawberries (or use three store-bought ones). Mash them in a ceramic or wooden bowl. Smear the pulp onto the face and neck and leave in place until the pack has dried completely. Rinse the skin in lukewarm spring water and pat dry.

BANANA

Banana is part of the plantain family and is rich in starches. It is phallic in shape and so has magical connections with sexual power and virility. A flower essence made from the blossoms of the fruit can help to treat male sexuality problems and will increase sensuality in men generally. Bananas can be used by men in talismanic magic, by carrying dried bananas in a pouch.

FIG

The fig tree is far more likely to have been the original tree in the Garden of Eden, according to current scholarship. (It is believed it was later changed to be the apple tree.) Its biblical connections are as famous as the olive branch and the vine. The Old Testament (see *Isaiah*) outlines the use of figs in the treatment of mouth problems and inflammation. The fig is sacred to Ishtar and Juno Lucina and can be given as an offering on the love altar when working with these two aspects of the goddess.

APPLE

The wild apple (crab apple) is most closely related to all aspects of love magic. The ancient festivity of wassailing (see pages 122–3) around the apple orchards is in praise of the love goddess and her gift of this wonderful fruit. An apple cut widthwise across the middle, reveals a five-pointed star (pentacle) at the center, making it a very magical, life-giving fruit. Wind the stalk of an apple fruit and gently try to puncture the fruit with it while repeating the letters of the alphabet. When the stalk penetrates the apple, the letter you have just recited is the first letter of the name of the person who will be important in your personal life at this particular time.

BLACKBERRY

Rubbing cuts and scratches with fresh blackberry leaves will stop the bleeding. Blackberries have excellent regenerative qualities, especially of the mucous membranes of the body. This fall fruit is a friend of the young oak trees, providing shelter to the saplings, and is also known as "the oak mother."

PEACH

The peach has been popular as an aphrodisiac for thousands of years. It represents long life, sincerity, and honesty. Originating in China, it was considered the sacred tree of the goddess. It is depicted in Taoist teachings as symbolizing the female genitals.

POMEGRANATE

The pomegranate, with its many seeds and red flesh, symbolizes the womb. It is sacred to Juno and is used in fertility magic.

LEFT Juno is associated with the fleshy pomegranate.

LEFT Blackberries can act as a tonic for the digestive system.

LOVE STONES

Several crystals are associated with Venus and can be carried or called upon for love magic. These include rose quartz, rosy (or strawberry) quartz, emerald, ruby, jade, peridot, malachite, and lodestone.

RUTILATED QUARTZ

Also known as the Venus Hair Stone because of the slivers of rutile-forming patterns within a clear quartz crystal, this crystal is traditionally considered the stone of the love goddess. It is linked to love because of its associations with the golden hair of the goddess. Carry a Venus Hair Stone when wishing to harmonize relationships or to call for the appearance of a lover.

ROSE AND ROSY QUARTZ.

These two crystals are particularly associated with clearing and healing the heart of old wounds associated with the past, allowing for release of pains and hurts associated with love. Their color brings the gentle pink rays into being, as supportive, nourishing, and cleansing.

RIGHT *Rose quartz.*
FAR RIGHT *Rough ruby.*

EMERALD

The emerald is said to have been brought to Earth from the planet Venus. Because it is green, it holds deep associations with the heart chakra. It is a stone of constancy in love, and it has the ability to reveal the faithfulness of a lover by clouding over in the company of infidelity.

ABOVE LEFT *Clear quartz.*
ABOVE RIGHT *Rough emerald.*

RUBY

Ruby is also known in India as the king of precious stones, as it has myriad positive qualities associated with love and success. It can bring desires into reality and it acts as a powerful heart protector, while drawing love toward you. Carry a ruby when you need strength and resolve during relationships, or when seeking good luck in love.

JADE

Jade has been held as sacred by the Chinese for thousands of years. Its qualities are said to be derived from the celestial dragon who held the seeds of life and carried them as jade to the center of the earth. Jade is found in two varieties: Jadeite, which is dark green, and Nephrite which is pale. Jade has also been used for love amulets by the Mayans, Egyptians, Aztecs, and Maoris, as they consider it to be full of celestial magic and vitality.

PERIDOT

Peridot is a green stone, so it has associations with the heart chakra and with love. It is an emotional balancer and protector and can be worn magically to draw the attentions of a lover. It can also calm jealous feelings, alienate anger, reduce stress, and promote growth through change.

MALACHITE

Malachite is another green stone that is also associated with the heart chakra and love. All green stones have the ability to harmonize inner and outer environments. This stone is sacred to Juno, and is also known as the peacock stone. Three-sided amulets are carved from malachite, possibly to represent the triple aspect of the goddess. In the past, malachite has been used to treat infertility.

ABOVE *Malachite.*
LEFT *Peridot.*

LODESTONE

The lodestone has magnetic qualities. When a pair of stones, one male and one female, is kept together, it can be used to draw a lover into your life. The lodestone is often employed in love magic in this way. It also attracts positive vibes and repels any that are negative.

RIGHT *A lodestone.*

LOVE AFFIRMATIONS

We often limit ourselves in our personal relationships because of past experiences, negative conditioning, or because we do not fit the "body beautiful" image that is so in vogue in the Western world.

To love another, it is important to first learn how to love yourself. An excellent way to find more self-worth and self-respect is by changing the negative program we have developed over many years with positive affirmations. Affirmations can be repeated every time a negative thought comes to mind, and can also be thought or spoken several times a day to program the mind to be positive.

An affirmation is a word or phrase that is positively charged with the qualities or attributes that we would like to possess but find difficult to access from within. If something you dislike about your body has been reaffirmed by your experiences in society (e.g. you cannot find clothes to fit you when you go shopping) you may begin to feel fat, ugly, and unacceptable as you are. Affirmations can help

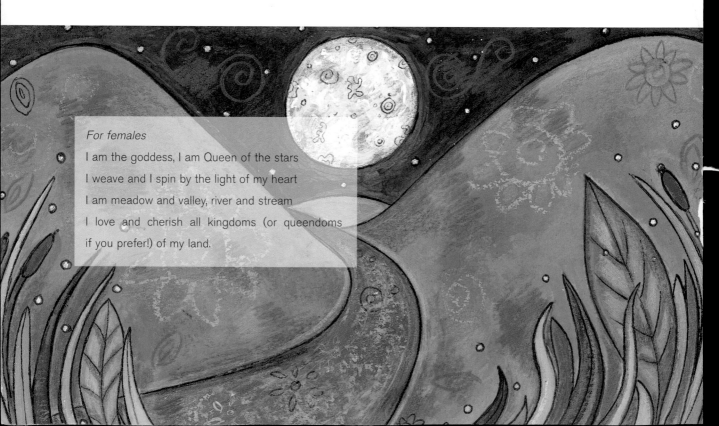

For females

I am the goddess, I am Queen of the stars
I weave and I spin by the light of my heart
I am meadow and valley, river and stream
I love and cherish all kingdoms (or queendoms if you prefer!) of my land.

First cast your circle of love. Working outside on a sunny day and beginning at about 11 am, sprinkle the flowers and leaves in a circle on the ground in a clockwise direction, saying: "I call the Great Spirit of all life into this sacred circle, that it may be blessed with boundless love and beauty. No harm may enter here." Make sure that a complete circle has been formed.

Place the bowl in the center of the circle and pour in spring water until it is one-third full. Sprinkle rose petals on the surface of the water and then the three elderflower heads. Leave the infusion in direct sunlight for three hours. Half fill the dropper bottle with vodka (to preserve the liquid). Strain the infusion through the fine cheesecloth and then pour it into the dropper bottle. Add seven drops each of wisteria and wild rose flower essence. Top up the bottle with spring water.

Take seven drops from the bottle daily for just over one month, beginning the night before a full moon and ending on the full moon the following month. To be most potent, perform this ritual when the moon is in one of the water signs – Cancer, Pisces, or Scorpio.

MYRTLE

Myrtle has been considered a flower of the gods – specifically Aphrodite and Venus – for thousands of years. It is said to have many magical qualities that include the ability to communicate with the otherworld, detect witches, communicate with departed souls, and bring harmony in marriage. It is often worn as a headdress to bestow magical gifts upon the wearer, and its name is also associated with the female reproductive organs.

PASSIONFLOWER

The passionflower symbolizes the passion of union between the male and the female forces. It is also employed in homeopathic remedies as "passiflora" to calm and soothe restlessness and intensity.

WISTERIA

Petite Fleur wisteria flower essence is a heart tonic that restores the ability to feel more in touch with the natural world, and opens the heart to experience the giving and receiving of unconditional love. It reminds us of "loving feelings" that are always there for us to enjoy.

WILD ROSE

Harebell wild rose essence is a gentle, soft, and warm essence that encourages a sense of contentment, building up confidence in our sensual nature and encouraging identification with our sexuality in a light-hearted and open way.

LOVE BATHING AT SACRED WELLS

ABOVE *Many ancient civilizations added oils or milk to water to beautify themselves.*

In ancient cultures, women would visit sacred wells to cleanse themselves and to ask for favors from the goddess, and once a year would spend time clearing and consecrating the area in preparation for the year to come. Seek out your nearest well, by looking on maps for names such as Holywell – or Holwell, for example, and then exploring the area to see if the well is still in existence. If it isn't, the ceremony can be performed at a lake, stream, or river, as all water sites are sacred to the love goddess.

To honor the spirit of water, take some flowers to her, such as water lily blossom, magnolia flowers, orange blossom, or roses. A simple and yet enchanting gift is to make a garland of daisies as a daisy chain, so often made by children. The daisy is a sacred flower of Venus and so makes a sweet and humble offering to her.

Traditionally, well cleansings and dressings would have been performed on May Day (May 1) or forty days after Easter on Ascension Day. To continue our ancestors' tradition, choose one of these days for your water blessing ceremony.

You will need:

container / bag to remove any local garbage

container of spring water

a towel

rose water

Stand at the edge of the water and announce your arrival to the local devas (flower spirits), dryads (tree spirits), and fairy folk by saying:

"Hail to thee, spirits of this place. I come in peace

ABOVE *Running water can prepare you for what love may bring.*

and ask permission to enter your sacred space in order to honor the Goddess of Love and Beauty. I ask you to bid me welcome."

Wait for a few moments until you hear the rustling of leaves or receive a similar sign to indicate that they have heard you, and then proceed by making your offering to the water goddess.

Before commencing, look around you to ensure that the area is clean, clear, and free from debris. Remove anything that is harmful to wildlife or potentially polluting to nature, and put it into the rubbish bag. Rinse your hands with spring water.

Place your flower offering gently upon the water and say the following dedication:
"Our Lady of the Waters, this offering I make to you.

May this simple act call your blessings here. Please cleanse me and sanctify me with your loving touch."

Imagine the whole area filling with light and love, as you become a channel for the love energy. Bathe your hands and feet in the water, visualizing yourself being cleansed and purified by the love goddess. If possible and personally preferred, submerge your whole body in the water. (Take care not to offend local people, and be certain that the water is unpolluted.)

Dry yourself and anoint your hands and feet with the rosewater (or your whole body if you submerged it). Stand by the water's edge and say "Thank you" to the water goddess and then to the spirits of the place. Leave the place with gentleness and gratitude in your heart for what you have experienced.

LOVE BATHING AT HOME

All water can be blessed and sanctified before use, including that used for bathing and showering at home. Before you begin, say the invocation to the water goddess as outlined on pages 78–9, imagining the bathroom filling up with light and love.

Charge the water with the herbs and flowers of love by making a packet that will scent your bath and help to connect you to loving vibrations. You can ritually bathe in this way before meeting a lover, or when working on loving yourself.

You will need:

a handful of medium oatmeal
a handful of lavender flowers
1 level tsp of orris root
3 drops of lavender essential oil
2 drops of palmarosa essential oil
1 drop of ginger essential oil
7in/17.5cm square of cheesecloth
green thread
a ceramic bowl

Place the oatmeal, lavender flowers, and orris root in the bowl and mix together. Add the essential oils and mix thoroughly. Place them on the square of cheesecloth and gather up the four corners. Tie the packet with the green thread, and hang it under the running bath water. Once the bath is run, place the packet into the water while you are bathing, visualizing love coming into your heart.

To be really decadent, sprinkle the water with rose petals, magnolia flowers, orange blossoms, sweet peas, and geranium leaves (or a chosen combination of these). Then luxuriate in the water for as long as you wish. Anoint your body with rosewater or orange flower water when your body is dry.

OATMEAL

Oats are sacred to Demeter, the goddess of grains, and are an aspect of the love goddess as provider and nourisher of life. Oats exfoliate the skin, providing a gentle scrub that removes dead cells and leaves the skin glowing.

LAVENDER

Lavender is often employed in love spells to help a wish to come true. It has the ability to wash away emotional conflict with its calming and soothing nature. It increases intuition and assists with issues of shyness and self-consciousness.

PALMAROSA

Palmarosa is an affordable substitute for rose absolute and is often used in love magic in place of rose essence. It accentuates the romantic, and is stimulating for men. It particularly lifts the senses, and clarifies thinking and focus. Palmarosa (like rose) has the ability to heal wounds of the heart and to open the heart in a gentle and supportive way.

GINGER

Ginger is a sexual tonic, invigorating to the sexual organs and inviting in its smell. It can increase sexual vitality and is arousing and warm. Ginger root can be carried by men to increase their sexual potency and a ginger tea is simple to make. Cut a thin slice of fresh ginger root and place in a large cup or mug. Pour boiling water over and leave to infuse for 5–10 minutes. Sweeten with honey if desired.

ORRIS ROOT

Orris root is derived from Iris florentina and is also known as "Love Root." It is used in love spells to attract love. The iris was named after the Greek rainbow goddess because it is found in many colors. Orris root has an aroma similar to violets.

ABOVE *You can make your own lover's packets by combining any herbs, spices, and fragrances of love that appeal to you.*

THE SUMMER LOVE GARDEN

The summer garden of love is filled with beauty, abundance, color, and wonderful fragrances. The principle love flower of this season is the rose in all its varieties, a bloom which is particularly associated with Venus, and lovers generally. Several other flowers of the heart include the daisy, magnolia, sweet pea, thyme, tansy, passionflower, myrtle, geranium, iris, lemon verbena, heather, meadowsweet, spearmint, yarrow, elder, and hibiscus.

To dedicate an area of your garden to the love goddess, plant the flowers of love, then add seashells, or love crystals such as rose quartz, and perhaps even a fountain or water feature. If you do not have a garden, a nice and simple idea is to plant a love pot (see pages 84–5). Choose the flowers or herbs that appeal to you and then add charms, ribbons, and decorations to the pot while thinking of love coming into your life.

ROSE

The rose is probably the flower most commonly associated with love and the love goddess. It was known as the "flower of Venus" in Roman times, which gives us an idea of how it was regarded. The red rose represents passion; the white rose, purity; the pink rose, tender love.

SWEET PEA

The sweet pea is the friendship flower – pretty, welcoming, and sweet-smelling, it encourages a sense of joy and happiness and can be used when calling for new friends.

HIBISCUS

Hibiscus is a warm, inviting, and exotic flower associated particularly with women. It has the ability to arouse female sexuality and helps women to accept and integrate their sensuality.

MEADOWSWEET

Meadowsweet has a musky fragrance similar to that of the elderflower. Also known as Lady of the Meadow, it was one of three herbs sacred to the Druids. A flower of the love goddess, it encourages happiness, dispels depression, and brings relaxation and peace. Its flowers, steeped in an infusion, provide a useful tonic for the digestive system.

THYME

Thyme is a sacred herb of Venus that is employed as a cleanser, and it also prevents nightmares. Its powerful scent when burned or crushed will invigorate and stimulate mind and body.

SPEARMINT

Spearmint is another herb of Venus. It has cooling and soothing qualities, and can be added to love spells, potions, and brews quite safely. Spearmint is also employed in healing rituals.

YARROW

Yarrow is one of the more magical plants of the love goddess. A powerful psychic stimulant, its stalks are used in casting the *I-Ching* oracle. It is used in love spells to encourage bonding and to attract a lover.

ABOVE *The rose is the flower most often associated with love and lovers.*

LOVE POTS

First decide which flowers or herbs you wish to grow, then choose an appropriate-sized pot. The variety of pots illustrated will inspire your own ideas.

The summer garden of love is filled with beauty, abundance, and wonderful fragrances. The principle flower during this season is the rose, which is particularly associated with Venus, and lovers generally. Several other flowers of the heart include the daisy, magnolia, sweet pea, thyme, tansy, passionflower, myrtle, geranium, iris, lemon verbena, heather, meadowsweet, spearmint, yarrow, elder, and hibiscus. You may like to have an area of your garden dedicated to the love goddess. This can be done by planting the flowers of love, and adding seashells, or love crystals such as rose quartz, and perhaps even a fountain or water feature, goddess statue or stone. If you do not have a garden, a nice and simple idea is to plant a love pot. Choose the flowers or herbs that appeal to you personally and then add charms, ribbons, and decorations to the pot while thinking of love coming into your life.

Cazzie, the love-pot-maker here, has made a variety of pots to bring some inspiration to your own ideas. Her basic ingredients for all the pots included brushes, a craft knife, strong glue, scissors, terra-cotta pots, and decorative items.

For the verdigris love pot you will need:
Terracotta pot of appropriate size
quick-drying clay
clear glue, old toothbrush
brown shoe polish
pthalo green and white acrylic paints
bronze wax crayon, water to thin

Cut out from the clay the required number of hearts. Fix onto the pot with strong, clear glue. Press them on with an old toothbrush to add a roughened texture to the surface of the hearts. Leave to dry. Apply polish to the pot to create a bronze effect. Leave to dry for about forty-eight hours. Remove any excess polish. Paint over the whole pot with a mixture of green and white acrylic paint, thinned with water. Wipe off any excess paint, until the desired verdigris finish is achieved. Coat the pot with a matt varnish. Leave to dry completely. Rub over the hearts with a bronze wax crayon, to give them a slightly coppery tone. Your pot is now ready for planting and you can choose whichever plant you like, and which is the most appropriate one for you.

ABOVE *Create your own pots using any charms, symbols, or colors of the love goddess that attract you.*

SUMMER CRAFTS

A STAFF TO THE
GODDESS OF LOVE

The staff is highly symbolic of male energy and of the creative force.
A staff is often seen carried by the wise ones, as far back as Moses and beyond.
The flowering staff of Joseph of Arimathea is said to blossom even today in
Glastonbury, Somerset in the UK, where it is known as the Holy Thorn. The staff is
translated as a wand in the tarot and represents the fire element. Making a staff to the
goddess of love is primarily for males to undertake in order to honor and respect her.
Carry the staff during magical ceremonies and at times when you need strength
and purpose.

❖

The craftworker Rag's journey took him to the woods near to a stream. It was a
summer Sunday and Rag asked the dryads (tree spirits) to help him in his
search. He was led to a sacred grove by a field. Hanging from an old
grandfather oak was a large branch that had broken off in a storm.
Rag burned some sacred herbs and asked if this was the
staff he was to take:

Sweet shaking staff of high summer sun,
Come from tree to me and let us be one.
Spirit of the tree, will you come with me
and move across the land?
Will you come and dance and
sing and chant in the ways
we understand?
Will you talk with me and help
me see nature in all her eternity?

Come be my staff of righteousness,
My support and source of
sweet excess,
My tree staff of power and desire,
My earth tower of creative fire.

A strong wind rose and Rag looked up to see the letter "Y" in the tree, which he took to mean yes. This meant that he could use that tree. Rag held the branch and communed with the oak spirit, and the hawk brothers came to circle overhead. The staff had been blessed and passed to him as a magical staff. If you travel to your own staff with respect and sincerity, magic will happen for you too.

RIGHT *The life force that flows through a staff gives support to the bearer. From the depths of the mother land the current of love rises up through the staff and is received through the hand directly to the heart.*

To make a staff you will need:

a piece of suitable wood
knife
chisel
coarse and fine sandpaper
clear varnish

Remove the bark and any stray branches from the main staff, using a chisel and a knife. Then sensitively smoothe it with coarse and fine sandpaper. Once the main body is finished, decorate it with any natural objects that you feel drawn to.

Rag secured a natural gourd to a branch point at the top using a craft bandage coated with plaster. He then attached thirteen pine cones and horns into place using the same method. Once the plaster had set, it was painted with green paint as a background to the seeds, which were attached with clear glue. Green and yellow material was tied and glued into place to form the headdress on the back of the gourd, then colored green and gold; cotton and wool was tied to the cones to represent Venus's hair. Green ribbon was glued around the wood and bells hung from the horns.

HOOP OF LOVE

The circle represents eternity, having no beginning and no end. Symbolizing the circle of life, it can be adapted to fit any cycle, and to signify union. It can also be called upon ceremonially, by casting a magic circle, to make a separation between the outer and inner world.

Weaving into a circle is a powerful form of magic, and is true of this hoop of love. As you weave, sing or listen to love songs, while calling for someone to love who will share their love with you.

You will need:

a plain ring 5 in/12.5cm or 10 in/25cm diameter, available from florists (or for stockists see page 124)
thin green silk ribbons
green silk thread
love charms, such as silver doves, swallows, peacock feathers, crystal beads, heart shapes
a variety of pink and green glass beads

Cover the basic hoop shape with the thin green ribbon, gluing it in place at the beginning and end. Knot the green thread to the top of the hoop. Moving clockwise around the hoop, make six points of a star. Work the thread over the front of the hoop, under the back, and over the thread, pulling tightly as you go, until there are six knots around the edge. Take the thread back to the starting point and fix it in place with a knot, to make a seven-pointed star shape. Go round once more, threading between the original knots six times all the way round, then return to the starting point.

Decorate your Hoop of Love as you like. The hoop illustrated is garnished with everlasting flowers to signify eternal love, a clay heart shape, colored feathers, and clay beads. The center of any circle is the most powerful point. It is therefore a good idea to attach a hanging charm that represents love to you in the middle.

To attach the feathers: for each one take three beads that are large enough to accommodate the end of the feather. Take a length of green thread and double it over to make a loop. Put it behind the hoop and then thread the two loose ends through the loop to secure the thread onto the frame.

Thread the beads, then secure them with a knot. Feed the end of the feather into the bead holes. In the same way, attach a crystal, feather, beads, or charms to the other loose thread.

Hang your Hoop of Love by your bed, or perhaps at a window where the breeze can blow through it, thus carrying your love to the world.

A MAGIC MIRROR

A seven-pointed star, sacred to the love goddess, is set upon a circular disc, symbolic of the full moon. Seven is the number associated with the Planet Venus, the planet of love. The star and the circle combine the energies of the moon and Venus, manifesting by geometric design the forces of self-love through the doorway of this magic mirror.

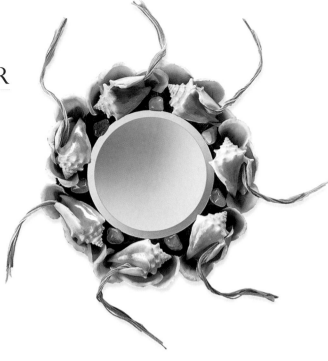

Between the points of the star are seven sea shells sacred to the goddess Aphrodite, Lady of Love in Greek mythology. From within each of the curves of the shells flow seven strands. There are forty-nine of these threads, forty-nine being the value of the word moon in English Qaballa. The shells are embraced by rose petals, the flower of love. Around the edge of the mirror are seven pieces of rose quartz, a crystal of the heart. These love stones lie upon a background of green, the color of our fertile earth. The reverse of the mirror symbolizes the evergreen of Mother nature and is studded with silver stars, reflecting the moonlit night. The sacred circumference of the mirror is sealed with ribbon and bows, suggestive of the "girdle of Venus."

The direction and energy of the shells and so the whole mirror itself is to the left (or moonwise),

left being the direction sacred to the female mysteries. This is a mirror of self-love, which gives the power of attraction. By gazing into it, the soul is filled with light.

You will need:

7in / 17.5cm circular disk

7in / 17.5cm seven-pointed star shape

craft glue

material to cover the mirror

7 silk rose petals (florists)

7 seashells (garden centers, beach shops, and craft supplies)

7 small rose quartz crystals

49 pieces of green thread

adhesive tape

ANIMAL TOTEMS	PLANTS & TREES	CRYSTALS	GENERAL
dove	rose	rose quartz	pink/green ribbons
bluebird	elderflower	jade	butterfly
bee	apple	malachite	copper wire
swan	daisy	emerald	hearts and cupids
deer	violet	peridot	sequins
duck	cherry	green stone	duck/swan feathers
			ladybird charms

decorative ribbon

5in/12.5cm circular mirror

(craft suppliers)

Cut a 7in-/12.5cm-diameter circular disk and a seven pointed star from ½in/1cm thick fiber board with a jigsaw or band saw, or ask your hardware store to do it for you. Secure the two pieces together with a strong craft glue and leave to dry. Cut a circular piece of your chosen material and glue it onto the face of the mirror, covering the star. Cut another circular piece of material, making sure that it is large enough to cover the back, and fold it up over the edge of the disk. Glue this into place, using an elastic band to hold it until the glue is set. Cut the rose petals from an artificial flower (available from garden centers and florists) and glue them into place between the points of the star. Glue the mirror onto the center of the star. Glue the shells onto the petals. Secure the pieces of rose

quartz onto the points of the star. Cut the lengths of thread and secure them at one end with a ball of adhesive tape, large enough to hold them in place when inserted into the shells. Finish the mirror by tying some ribbon around the edge.

On a Friday, at any time when the moon is between new and full, take some rose essential oil and anoint the ring finger of your left hand with three drops. Write the word "love" across the surface of the mirror with your finger. Soften your gaze and fill your heart with loving feelings. Send them into the mirror. Now imagine that love is returning to you from the mirror and bathe in the loving sensations.

Continue for as long as you feel a connection, which should be for about 15 minutes. It is advisable not to display your magic mirror, but to store it in a green silk or velvet cloth in a consecrated place when it is not in use.

A SUMMER LOVE RECIPE

This summer cordial blends the potent masculine forces of vibrancy, strength, and positivity contained within the orange, with the feminine lunar qualities of healing and purification found in the lemon. The two are also embraced by elderflower, a blossom of Venus and a sacred tree of the earth mother. The magical uses of elderflowers include divination, love magic, transformation, and protection. It is said that if you stand beneath an elder during a thunderstorm, you will not be struck by lightning.

Make this cordial during the new to full moon phase, ideally when the moon is passing through the signs of Libra or Taurus, because Venus is exalted in these signs, making the most of the powers of love.

When gathering the blossoms, remember to honor the spirit of the trees from which you remove the flowerheads. Stand next to your chosen trees and ask first before you cut the blossoms off. Explain that you will be making a summer love cordial and ask which blossoms would be best for you. Be guided by the tree to the blooms you are being given permission to take. Do not take twenty-five heads from a single tree, but from several trees in the area, to ensure continuance of life there. Thank the trees by leaving a strand of your hair upon each branch where you have removed some flowers. The best time to pick is coming up to midday on a dry day. Use only elderflower heads that have been picked from trees away from main roadways, to ensure that no excess pollution from vehicles has affected the blooms.

While making this cordial, visualize the bucket as a cauldron, into which you can pour your sacred wishes for love and joy. Imagine that you have the ability to create your universe as you stir the ingredients together. Stir for yourself, for your loved ones, and for your friends.

Wishing for others is a very rewarding act. You may like to make this cordial and give a bottle to each person you feel would benefit from some love and joy in their life, when it feels appropriate to do so. However, you must never tell of the magic that you have woven; if you do, then the cordial will lose its magical power.

ORANGE AND ELDERFLOWER
CORDIAL

You will need:

3 pints / 1.7 liters boiled spring water

a bucket

3lb / 1.3kg sugar

4 oranges

1 lemon

25 elderflower heads

2 oz tartaric acid

Boil the spring water and pour it into a plastic bucket. Leave it to cool slightly, then dissolve the sugar in it. Wash and slice the fruit and add them to the bucket. When the water has cooled, add the elderflowers and tartaric acid. Stir well and cover. Occasionally stir the mixture over the next twenty-four hours. Bottle the cordial in sterilized, dry screwtop bottles.

Dilute to taste with sparkling mineral water and serve with sprigs of spearmint and ice cubes.

ABOVE *The orange is a solar fruit and the lemon a lunar fruit.*

SEPTEMBER
TO NOVEMBER

A FALL ALTAR

The fall love goddess is represented by Demeter, the
goddess of corn, grain, and the harvest. At this time of year we reap
what we have sown, and harvest what we have planted throughout the year.
It is also the time when we must begin to let go of expectations, hopes, and
dreams that have not yet come to fruition. We must allow them to pass back into
the earth to rest, before the next cycle of the year begins.

❖

On your altar, place sheaves of rye, wheat, oats, and barley, together with apples,
blackberries, and plums. Burn orange or beeswax candles, and sprinkle cassia bark
or sandalwood onto hot charcoal. Set up your fall altar during a waning moon (directly on
or just after the full moon time). Your altar will be especially potent
if you lay it out on the eve of Lammas (August 1) or during the actual night
of the harvest full moon in September.

LETTING GO

Ceremonies that can be performed during the fall season involve giving thanks for the gifts of the year, and letting go of those things that either have not yet come to fruition or represent parts of yourself that you would like to release. This is an ideal time of the year to consider healing yourself and/or others, because it is the season of release, of letting go.

You will need:

orange or beeswax altar candles

menthol crystals or essential oil

a red candle

black pen

natural paper

heatproof bowl

Place all the items on your altar. Light the altar candles and burn menthol crystals or essential oil in an aromatherapy burner. Just after the full moon, stand facing west. Hold your left hand out with the index and middle fingers extended, and cast a circle around yourself by saying:

"Hail to the powers of the West! I stand before you and ask your protection and guidance. Open the gates and come to my aid." Turn north and say a

LEFT *The fall altar is one of abundance, where we can give thanks to the mother goddess.*

similar invocation for the north, then repeat for east and south. Then turn back to the west and say, "The circle is cast. By the powers of love, light, wisdom and truth, no harm may enter here." Place the red candle in the center of your cast circle and as you light it, say, "I call upon the sacred flame to purify, cleanse, and bless this ceremony."

While you carry out this ceremony, consider what you would like to be healed. It could be any negative emotion, situation, or circumstance in your life that appears to limit or bind you in some way. Think hard and make sure that this is something really important to you: give this ceremony the respect it deserves. Write down your thoughts – envy, doubt, anger. Walk widdershins (counterclockwise) five times around your circle, building up as much recognition of this emotion, situation, or circumstance as you can. Then light the paper from the red candle and drop it into the heatproof bowl. Make sure that the paper completely burns. Blow out all candles. Close your circle by facing south and saying, "Hail and farewell, powers of the South! Thank you for your presence." Turn east and say farewell and give thanks, then repeat for north and west. Then say, "This ceremony is done, the healing begins."

A FALL SPELL

No self-respecting magical practitioner is without thread and cord, for they have deep magical associations. The knot is made while focusing upon something of importance, in order to hold the energy in place. The cord (of various colors) is used in magic for initiation purposes as well as for casting moveable circles of protection. This particular spell can help to hold your wishes throughout the winter months.

Magic really does work. Whatever you ask for will come to you, so it is important to cleanse, prepare and purify yourself prior to any magical ceremony.

You will need:

3 beeswax candles

2 21in / 52.5cm length of thin green cord

(available from upholstery shops)

a 21 in / 52.5cm length of thin white cord

a 21 in / 52.5cm length of thin red cord

green thread

a small charm or gift to the goddess

(e.g. clay bead, silver charm, or muslin bag

filled with seeds – use your imagination)

representations of your wish

(e.g. crystals, beads, shells, charms, stones,

or words written on natural paper)

Begin by casting a circle around yourself (see page 97). Light the three beeswax candles while saying:

"Weaver of destiny, spinner of fate,
I ask you seal each knot I make.
Let love be woven here.
I ask you weave the red and white.
Let man and woman unite.
Let love be woven here."

Lay the green cord in the centre of the circle as you face it, with the red cord on one side and the white cord on the other. Tie the three cords together with a fastening knot, while visualizing that you are beginning your journey to a lover, and that he/she is also at the start of his/her journey to you.

Plait the cords together a short way and then stop. Focus on your wish as strongly as you can and then tie a knot in the cords, imagining that you are binding your wish into the cords. Plait a little further and then repeat your wish in the same way and tie another knot. Continue plaiting and knotting until there are six knots. Plait to the end of the lengths and then tie your seventh knot. Your seventh knot is the final knot and must be tied tightly, because if it comes undone the spell will not work effectively.

Using green thread, tie to the plait your charm or gift to honor the goddess of love while you repeat your thanks to her. Then tie on any totem, wherever you like, to empower your wish.

This spell is functional, so do not worry too much about the appearance of the plait. What is important is the amount of attention, care, and feeling that you put into its making. If the knots come undone at any time, perform the ceremony from the beginning again.

Bury the plait while asking the earth mother to hold your wishes so that they can grow strong again in the spring. Do not dig it up.

RIGHT *The red thread here symbolizes woman, the white thread, man. Both are bound together by the green thread of Venusian love.*

LOVE DIVINATION
WITH CRYSTALS

As well as being used for adornment, healing, personal growth and as energy enhancers, crystals can be used for divination as well.

Each crystal should ideally be as similar in size as possible, (not a bead, which is too round), and stored in a black velvet pouch when not in use. For this divination pack you will need:

a square piece of black velvet cloth

1 amethyst

1 lapis lazuli

1 blue lace agate

1 peridot

1 citrine

1 carnelian

1 obsidian

1 bloodstone – negative – no stone

1 turquoise – positive – yes stone

Each crystal has a specific meaning which can be interpreted as part of the spread, depending upon where it falls in relation to the others. As with all forms of divination, the more you practise the easier it becomes, to read the messages.

Before you start, it is important to make a link with each crystal in your divination pack by sitting with each one respectfully before using them.

Rub all the crystals in your hands for a few seconds, while thinking of the question you have in mind. Throw them onto the cloth, noting where they fall in relation to the yes and no stones. If it is hard to distinguish whether the yes or no stone is closest to any of the other stones, your question cannot be answered at the moment. The nearest stone to either the yes or no stone is the most significant for the reading.

AMETHYST

Violet stone, associated with the crown chakra. If it is nearest to the yes stone – a spiritual opportunity, peace; no stone – any action will produce stress.

LAPIS LAZULI

Dark blue stone, associated with the third eye chakra. Change is imminent. If it is nearest to the yes stone – an answer will show itself soon; nearest to the no stone – change is not imminent.

BLUE LACE AGATE

Blue stone, associated with the throat chakra. Communication is indicated. A fresh start or new opportunity will present itself. A time of learning. If it is nearest to the yes stone – making contact is favorable; nearest to the no stone – contact is not advised.

PERIDOT

Green stone, associated with the heart chakra. Emotional issues, deep love, creative powers, and friendship are highlighted. Give as you would like to receive. If it is nearest to the yes stone – act positively; nearest to the no stone – emotions could run high.

CITRINE

Clear yellow stone, associated with the solar plexus chakra. Progress can be made if you are not hurried. Keep forcefulness in check and don't make assumptions. The future looks bright if caution is taken. Mental attitudes and business partners are also highlighted. If it is nearest to the yes stone – a productive result; nearest to the no stone – check your attitudes, and work on yourself before proceeding.

CARNELIAN

Orange stone, associated with the belly chakra. Choices need to be made, marriage or a union is possible, but be clear about what you want. If it is nearest to the yes stone – union is strongly indicated; nearest to the no stone – not a wise moment to move any closer, and you should clear your past of personal debris.

OBSIDIAN

Black stone, associated with the base chakra. If it is nearest to the yes stone – be practical, realistic, and true to yourself whatever that may be; if it is nearest the no stone – not the time to act, but to keep silent and wait. Fear and/or confusion could cloud correct judgement.

HEALING WATERS

The water element on the wheel of love lies in the west. Water has powerful healing potential. Develop a relationship with the undines (water elementals), who can assist with a water healing, by sitting quietly next to water and announcing your presence to them. Say that you come in peace, to share time with them. Ask them to show you the spirit of water, to let you feel the essence of water within yourself, and to assist you with the healing ceremony.

A RELEASING USING WATER

For a "healing waters" cleansing you will need:

running water (stream, brook, river, sea)

a small clear quartz crystal
as an offering to the undines

a flat stone

a non-toxic water soluble fiber-tip pen
(a child's pen is ideal)

Hold the quartz crystal to your heart, and say the following prayer:

"Great spirit, I ask for blessings upon the undines, for those beings who keep our waters cleansed and purified. I offer this crystal to those of the water kingdom, as a token of my love and respect."

Throw your crystal gently into the water.

Now hold the stone to your heart, and say the following invocation:

"Grandfather, grandmother rock, I ask for your assistance. I ask that you take the words which I shall write upon you and carry them to the water spirits for cleansing and release. I am thankful for your wisdom, I am thankful for your help."

Using a fiber-tip pen, write clearly and briefly on the stone whatever it is that you wish to release from your life (e.g. "irritability with loved ones," "insecurity," or perhaps "the pain of parting with x"). Your choice of words should state what it is that you wish to cleanse and purify about yourself, as opposed to what you wish to develop in yourself.

 Stand by the water's edge, and visualize that everything written on the stone is being drawn out of you and into the stone itself, and from the stone into the words that are written on it. Call to the undines to watch for your stone as you drop it gently into the water, by saying the following invocation:

"Water sprites, beings of the flowing way,
Watch over my stone and the words thereon.
Cleanse the heart of she/he who wrote upon it.
With dancing water, let the condition be gone."

Continue standing there for a short while, visualizing the undines coming to your stone to help you release whatever is stopping you from flowing with the tides of life. You may even be visited by a jumping fish or a swan, as an acknowledgement from the water kingdom. As you turn away, have gratitude in your heart for the help that you will receive, but do not look back to the point where you dropped your stone in the water.

A FALL LOVE POTION

The fall harvest brings richness and abundance as crops ripen and are gathered and food is plentiful. However, it is also a time to let go and release those things that have not come to fruition – to prune and cut back unnecessary expectations, wants, or desires. It is a time of preparation, of being aware of what is needed for the time ahead, much as the natural world prepares itself for the long cold winter months ahead. This love potion is one of release, and also of re-connecting with the earth. It will help to ground and settle personal issues that need more time before they can re-emerge in a positive way. Think of these things when you are making your fall love potion.

You will need:

a small bowl of earth

10 ml stopper bottle (available from drugstores)

fresh peppermint leaves

miniature bottle of vodka

azurite gem essence (from Korte Flower Essences)

apple (from Masters Flower Essences)

blueberry pollen flower essence

(Alaskan Flower Essences)

cornflower essence (from Flower Essence Society)

spring water

Place the bowl of earth in the center of your altar. Then, stand the empty stopper bottle in the bowl of earth. Now make a circle around the bowl out of single peppermint leaves, with the leaf stalks facing away from the center of the circle. As you place each leaf in its particular place, try and think of something that you would like to release (e.g. sadness, fear of intimacy, or getting out of an old relationship), and call, "Goddess of love, fill this circle with your healing heart."

Pour vodka into the stopper bottle until it is one-third full. Add to the bottle seven drops of each essence in this order: azurite, apple, blueberry pollen, cornflower. Top up the bottle with spring water and shake it gently. Label the bottle "releasing remedy" with the date clearly marked.

Take seven drops in a glass of spring water daily for one month. Discard the contents after one month. Keep the remedy in a cool, dry place away from electrical appliances.

AZURITE

Azurite gem essence is used for releasing past or outmoded habits, beliefs, opinions, and attitudes that are no longer helpful. It has the ability to attract the light of clarity for cleansing both the mind and body.

APPLE

Apple flower essence can be taken at any time when there is emotional tension, e.g. unhappiness, dissatisfaction, or anxiety. It helps to restore a positive outlook, while releasing any negative state of mind. It enhances a happy and healthy attitude to life.

BLUEBERRY POLLEN

Blueberry pollen is an Alaskan flower essence used for releasing deeply ingrained patterns of behavior, and for assisting with the process of letting go to gain a richer and more abundant attitude to life.

CORNFLOWER

Cornflower essence assists the grounding and releasing process. It is useful when you are in a chaotic urban environment and yearn for the peace of a more natural setting. It can also be used for connecting to the earth mother, in order to ground, stabilize, and orient yourself to the earth's energies.

RIGHT *Earth is a powerful healer, having the ability to transform old patterns into new potentials.*

A FALL CRAFT

WEB OF DEMETER

Traditionally, fall is a time to give thanks to the goddess for providing food for
the table. On each farm the last sheaf of corn would be made into a corn dolly
that would be stored to ensure a home for the goddess until the following year. In the
same spirit, this magical craft can be offered as a home for the goddess over the winter
season. This craft can be made indoors, and if it is woven in the field or meadow,
it will build a strong link with the domain of the love goddess.

Threads and cords in mythology represent the umbilical cord, and so the symbolic
return to the womb before emerging reborn. The weaving of threads can lead
humanity back through the maze of life to mystical initiation and understanding.
Women, especially, have great power as weavers, which can be called upon
when weaving this Web of Demeter.

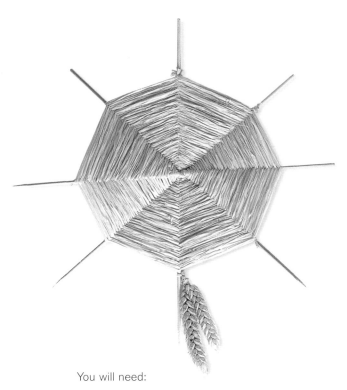

You will need:

4 long wooden skewer sticks

natural raffia

scissors

heads of oats, barley, rye, or wheat

decorative charms and feathers

First prepare yourself by bathing and cleansing in water, to which you have added six drops of rose geranium essential oil. Firmly bind two sticks to make a cross, using a length of raffia. Place another stick in the spaces made by the two sticks and bind it tightly. Then add the final stick to make eight spokes coming from a central point. Eight is the number of spider woman — the most proficient weaver of us all. Her eight legs represent the four directions and the four elements.

Moving clockwise, begin weaving the raffia around the sticks following the illustration, to build a web pattern around the sticks. As you weave, imagine that the goddess is entering the threads, and that you are creating a home for her until the spring. Weave with love and beauty in your heart; weave with gratitude. Continue weaving until there is about 1in/2.5cm from the ends. Fasten the raffia with a knot at the back of the web.

Take three heads of your chosen crop and bind them together with a piece of raffia. Attach them to the base spoke of the web. The basic structure of the web is now complete, and ready to be decorated. Use any of the following charms or representations: lapis lazuli, a dove charm or feathers, roses, a fish charm, a dolphin, a white sow, an ant, a bee, little hand-made loaves of bread, corn, all seeds, six-petalled flowers, a diamond shape, a mermaid, magpie feathers, or pearls.

With this Web of Demeter, you could choose to represent the goddess as earth mother, with beads in the colors of the fall earth (ocher, olive, orange, and gold), and the shibboleth (sacred corn). I remembered Demeter's bountiful ability to feed her children with loaves from our blessed land while making the web.

ABOVE *Weaving is a sacred art and is especially potent when performed by women.*

FALL SEED BREAD

Fall is a good time to start baking your own bread. You can use it as a time to celebrate all the good things that come out of the earth and come to fruition during this season. Many harvest festival displays include a wheatsheaf as a central icon, and it is often made of bread. Your own loaves help to celebrate the earth mother and her efforts.

When working magically with cookery, it is important to use ingredients that are as natural as possible, preferably organic products. Organic produce contains more potency than non-organic because it carries more of the earth's vibrant energy and so will not only increase any magical effectiveness, but will also ensure the nutritional value of it.

You will need:

8 fl oz / 225ml of spring water

3 tsp dried yeast

3 tsp brown sugar

1 lb / 900g whole-wheat flour

2 oz / 50g organic oats

5 tbsp sunflower seeds

5 tbsp pumpkin seeds

3 tbsp sesame or walnut oil

soya milk

Boil the water, then pour it into a mixing bowl and leave it to cool until just warm. Add the yeast and sugar and stir to dissolve. Leave the mixture to stand in a warm place until the water is frothy and the yeast activated. Add the remaining ingredients, and stir well with a wooden spoon in a clockwise direction until they form a dough. Cover the dough with a polythene bag and leave to stand in a warm place for between 45 minutes and 1 hour, or until it has risen. Put the dough on a floured surface and knead and pummel it well, folding it over and working it with your hands. As you work the dough, recall the fields where the grains and seeds have come from, and consider the rains that moistened the earth and supported the sprouting grains. Give thanks for the miracles that life brings to your larder.

When the bread dough is well-kneaded, elastic and filled with your gratitude, divide it into two. Form each into a round: one for the goddess of grains and one for you. Leave it in a warm place to rise again. Then brush the top with soya milk and sprinkle some seeds on the top. Bake in the middle of the oven at 400°F/200°C/Gas Mark 6 for about 35–40 minutes. To check if it is cooked, tap the bottom of the bread: it should sound hollow. Leave it to cool on a wire rack.

HARVEST OFFERING

Take the loaf that you have baked for the goddess of grains to a wild place. Stand and make your presence known to the local spirits and say that you come in peace to give something back to the earth mother. Break your bread into four pieces and scatter them to each of the four directions – west, north, east, then south – with deepest thanks in your heart for what you have received. Say whichever prayer feels right for you.

If you cannot get to a wild place, put the bread on a bird table, feed it to the ducks at the local pond, or simply lay it on your altar as an offering, but do not eat it yourself. If you go to a Lammas ceremony, throw your offering into the fire there.

ABOVE *All seeds and grains are very symbolic of the harvest goddess.*

DECEMBER
TO FEBRUARY

A WINTER ALTAR

The winter altar to love is one of an everlasting nature.
At this time of year evergreens such as holly and ivy are
traditionally displayed. Holly is a tree of Mars, and ivy is a plant of
Saturn. Traditionally, the two bound together were given to newly married
couples. Display evergreens around your altar and lay out your winter love
ingredients between the evergreens. These can include almonds, vanilla pods, licorice
root, red and green berries, mistletoe, pine cones and pine leaves (to represent Venus's
lover), and any dried herbs and spices of Venus such as allspice, marjoram, oregano,
and lemon verbena, plus red candles.

❖

Red berries and white berries represent the union of female (red) and male (white).
The red berries symbolize the blood of woman and the white berries symbolize the
seminal fluid of man. Binding the two together in ceremony will help to ensure
"everlasting" affection throughout the colder winter months.

A WINTER LOVE GARLAND

You will need:

a length of strong twine
floristry wires
evergreens of holly, ivy,
pine branches, mistletoe
red and white berries
red and green floristry ribbon
pine cones
(Mistletoe berries are poisonous, so do not take them
internally, and holly leaves can sometimes cause an
allergic reaction.)

Gather up bunches of the evergreens and fasten them with floristry wire. Make enough bunches to cover the length of twine you have chosen. Using floristry wire, attach each one to the twine. When the length is completely covered, use floristry wire to add bunches of red berries and white berries at intervals, and the pine cones. Tie ribbons along the length and fasten them in place with floristry wire. While you are weaving the garland, say the following invocation:

"King and Queen together be,
bound by love eternally.
King and Queen shall never part,
honored here with joyful heart."

Think of the men and women all over the world who are learning how to love and respect each other in all of their relationships — be it father, mother, son, daughter, sister, brother, lover, or friend. The following can also be included in your garland.

VANILLA PODS

Vanilla beans are derived from a Mexican orchid. This pod is often used in love spells to attract the attention of a lover. Pieces of the fresh bean can be added to love oils or to aromatherapy burners to arouse intimate feelings and sensuality.

LICORICE ROOT

Licorice has soporific qualities, having the ability to calm, soothe, and pacify. Carry licorice root when wanting to ensure smooth and trouble-free relations with a loved one.

MISTLETOE

Mistletoe is a favorite choice at Christmas time for affectionate kissing. This tradition stems from ancient orgiastic fertility practices, where the berries of mistletoe (especially when grown upon the oak tree) were considered part of the oak god's semen. It has phallic connotations.

A WINTER LOVE INCENSE

When making this incense, remember to weave your heart into the ceremony.

This winter love incense is dedicated to the Sun (the masculine life-giver) and to Venus (the feminine lover), brought together by ingredients that will fill your home with loving vibrations during the winter season.

You will need:

ceramic pestle and mortar

2 parts (by weight) juniper berries

4 parts frankincense,

4 parts spearmint

1 part cloves

1 part cinnamon

storax to bind

5 drops palmarosa essential oil

4 parts colophony (pine resin) –

or substitute with pine needles

Place all ingredients, except the colophony or pine needles, into the mortar. Grind them together with a pestle, until they are the size of small peas. Add the colophony or pine needles. Sprinkle a pinch of the incense onto burning charcoal to raise health, happiness, and joy.

JUNIPER

Juniper is a cleansing and purifying solar herb (and one that is ruled by the sun), which is widely used in incenses that are burned during ceremonies held for different gods and goddesses. It has the ability to guide us to right action and practice, so leading the way to clearing what stands in the way of opening our hearts to love.

FRANKINCENSE

Frankincense is a solar fragrance, which blesses and sanctifies any area where it is burned. It is one of the most sacred aromas of the ancients, still gathered by the Somali people from the genus of Boswellia trees in Africa. It is a sweet-smelling resin which induces spiritual awareness and connects us to feelings of peace and harmony. It is also an ideal addition to any meditational mix. It is a very popular frangrance today.

SPEARMINT

Spearmint is sacred to the goddess of love. It has healing abilities, as well as associations with love. It is regularly burned or given as an offering during love ceremonies and also assists in building an abundant consciousness.

LEFT *Frankincense is still gathered at the Boswellia trees that grow in southern Africa.*

CLOVES

Cloves are associated with the sun and are often used when wanting to draw a lover closer. Derived from the unripe flowers of the Eugenia caryophyllata tree, they are harvested after the rainy season and have been imported into Europe since 400 CE as a culinary and medicinal spice.

CINNAMON

Cinnamon is obtained from the bark of the cinnamon tree and is highly aromatic. It is a solar spice which has a zest and life to it, and is a potentizer often used in love magic to invigorate and stimulate our passionate nature.

STORAX

Storax originates from a tree found in Asia Minor. Its resin is used as a binder for other incense ingredients. It has a heady vanilla scent and is also known as liquid amber.

PALMAROSA

Palmarosa oil can be used very effectively in place of rose absolute products, which are extremely expensive. Synthetic oils are always a poor substitute to the real, pure, thing when it comes to magical working, and so alternatives like pure palmarosa are always better. Palmarosa is a scented grass grown in India.

COLOPHONY

The pine tree is sacred to Adonis (Venus's lover). It is included in this incense mix to balance the male and female energies. Pine is also cleansing and protective, and as an evergreen symbolizes eternal life. Pine cones have long been used to represent fertility.

DREAMS OF A LOVER

You can have a significant influence over your dream state if you program your mind before going to sleep. Focus your mind on a particular question and then program yourself to remember the dreams. Keep a dream diary and pen by your bed, so that if you are woken up

BELOW *Gaia is the great mother goddess of the Earth, oracles, divination, and dreams.*

(which often happens after a psychic dream) you will be able to write it down immediately with clarity.

You can also make a magical offering to Gaia (a goddess of the dreamtime) to help bring you prophetic dreams about your future love, which will increase the potency of any request. Collect some laurel leaves and place them on your altar, and light green candles in her honor. Also display any fruits and flowers of love, especially barley grains (obtainable from most wholefood shops). If you are also making the Dreaming Heart Pillow, place your rutilated quartz crystal on the altar, too.

Sit before your altar. Bow your head with your hands held together at your heart, and say:

"Praise be to Gaia, Great Mother of this ancient land – I offer this laurel as a gift from a humble heart," and then point to the laurel offering.

Now open your hands and hold them, palms facing upward, and say:
"I call to you to bring to me a dream, to guide me to the temple of the heart, that in my dreams I meet my own true love. Once met, we need not be apart. This I ask for the highest good of all."

Sit in quiet meditation for up to twenty minutes, letting your mind be taken where it will, then gently bring yourself back to the present moment. It is important to thank Gaia before closing this ceremony. Do this by bowing your head as you did to open the ceremony, with your hands in the prayer position at the heart, and say "Thank you". Blow out the candles.

ANGEL	Spiritual happiness
SMALL BIRDS	Joy
CHERRIES	Joyful love
COAL FIRE	Harmony in the home
FRIENDLY DOG	Fidelity
DOVE	Good news
FAIRY	Your wish will come true
ROSE	Deep love
SKYLARK	Happy communication
LETTER	News is on the way
BEE	The love goddess hears your call
CANDLE FLAME	A blessing from the spirit world
HARP	Hope
NUTS	An opportunity to grow through adversity
OLIVE	A reunion
RABBIT	The relationship will grow stronger, have no fears
GIVEN A RING	Marriage
BROKEN RING	Broken relationship
FALLEN TREE	End of a relationship
CLEAR WATER	Emotional happiness
MURKY WATER	Emotional confusion
STORMY WATER	Emotional turmoil

INTERPRETATIONS OF LOVE DREAM SYMBOLS

The meanings to the subjects listed below are only guidelines. It is far better to meditate upon a dream, or wait for its meaning to reveal itself to you, than to rely upon static symbology. Use these items to guide you only until you become confident enough to trust your own interpretations.

ABOVE *Dreams can often bring hidden messages to the surface. It is well worth taking the time to try to understand them.*

A WINTER CRAFT

The ingredients for this pillow have been carefully
chosen to help you call for dreams about a lover or for prophetic
dreams about love in your future. As with all magical crafts, it should be
consecrated before use. You can adapt the quantities to suit your sense of
smell. Mugwort (*Artemisia vulgaris*) is a herb of Venus that is highly magical. It can
be used to consecrate magical equipment and to enhance their divinatory powers.

❖

Dittany (*Origanum dictammus*) is another herb of Venus that helps make a connection with
other planes of existence. It also helps develop psychic abilities, and is a useful aid to deep
meditation and vision-questing. Myrtle (*Myrica cerifera*) is associated with all love magic. It
represents fidelity and marriage, as well as symbolizing love and fertility. Wreaths of myrtle
can be worn when calling to Venus during love ceremonies. Dill seeds (*Anethum grave-
olens*) are protective and will ensure that dreams are sweet and restful. They are also
love-attractors in magical workings. Traditionally, dill as a herb was given to children
diluted in water to settle an upset stomach and help them to sleep. Jasmine oil
(*Jasminium officinale*) can enhance the clarity of dreams, and can also
draw dreams of spiritual love toward you.

A DREAMING HEART PILLOW

You will need:

natural light-colored green fabric

needle and thread

1 dessertspoon mugwort leaves

1 tablespoon dittany leaves

1 tablespoon myrtle leaves

1 heaped teaspoon dill seeds

3 drops jasmine essential oil

green thread

pink and green beads and symbols of Venus (optional)

First, cleanse, bless, and consecrate your herbs. Light white candles on your altar and then pass each of the herbs through the smoke of burning frankincense, saying:

"I cleanse, bless, and consecrate this herb in the name of all that is sacred. May it be empowered and blessed by the sweet goddess of herbs and flowers – the Lady Venus – for the highest good of all."

Keep your herbs upon your altar until you need them. Cut out two identical heart shapes from the fabric approximately 5in/13cm high. On the right side of one piece use tailor's chalk to draw the magic knot pattern. Stitch the pattern using straight stitch or, alternatively, sew beads to make up the pattern of your choice.

Attach any further love symbols, beads, and sequins to your design that may appeal to you. With two hearts right sides together, pin and then stitch the hearts three-quarters of the way around, leaving an opening at the top. Turn the fabric right side out and fill your dreaming heart pillow with the herbs. Sew up the opening. Before going to sleep, squeeze the pillow a few times and inhale the fragrance, and mentally call for the dream you require. Place it near to where you sleep, or under your pillow when you get into bed. Keep your dream heart on or under your altar when you are not using it for dreaming.

RIGHT *You can decorate your dreaming heart pillow with any personal love charms.*

WINTER LOVE RECIPES

ALMOND CRESCENTS

This delicious winter recipe can be decorated with shapes that
are sacred to the love goddess, such as hearts, stars, or fishes

❖

The word crescent is derived from *crescere* (to grow). The crescent shape is a very
ancient representation of the goddess. It also represents newness and purity, as well as
the regenerative potential of the feminine. It has powerful lunar connections, symbolizing
the beginning of a new lunar cycle. Winter is the power time of the moon and the feminine, and so these crescents can be made for the goddess with the request that, as the
old year passes, the new will bring continued life, health, and happiness.

To make the almond paste you will need:

2oz / 50g melted organic butter, 3oz / 75g superfine (caster) sugar

4oz / 100g organic ground almonds, 2 organic egg yolks

½tsp natural almond essence

1 tablespoon orange flower water

Place all the ingredients in a mixing bowl and mix together well, thinking of love, harmony, and happiness as you bind the ingredients. Chill the mixture in a refrigerator while you make the pastry.

For the pastry you will need:

8 oz / 200g organic all-purpose (plain) flour
1 / 2oz / 12g organic melted butter
3 tbsp orange flower water
3½ fl oz / 100ml cold spring water
pinch of salt

Sift the flour into a mixing bowl and add the salt. Make a well in the center and add the other ingredients. Using a knife, mix together until the dough begins to come together. Knead the dough on a floured surface until it is smooth and elastic, while again thinking of love and happiness. Let it rest for fifteen minutes.

Roll out the dough thinly on a floured surface. Cut out 3in/7.5cm circles. Place a piece of almond paste in the middle of each circle, then dampen the edges with water and fold over. Bend each piece into a crescent shape. Prick the crescents to prevent them bursting during cooking.

To decorate your crescents with shapes that are sacred to the goddess, cut out hearts, stars, and fishes from thin pastry, and then moisten one side with water. Press the shapes gently onto the top of each crescent.

Transfer the crescents to a non-stick baking sheet and bake for 15–20 minutes at 325°F/160°C/Gas Mark 3 until they are very pale golden brown. While they are still warm, sprinkle them with orange flower water and roll them in icing sugar.

Share almond crescents with all your loved ones to encourage warmth, love, and harmony with family and friends for the year ahead.

ORANGE BLOSSOM

Orange blossoms are traditionally given to couples in bridal bouquets, to ensure constancy in love. When made into an essential oil orange blossom is a subtle and delightful fragrance known as neroli. Neroli helps to bring joy, and is excellent for calming any fears that are based around starting a new sexual relationship, or continuing with one.

CIDER CUP

Wassailing is a traditional activity that originally took place on Old New Year's Eve (January 17) around the oldest tree in the apple orchard. The first cider crop was poured as a libation (offering) around her roots to thank the dryads (tree spirits) for the year's crop of apples, and as a way of asking for a good harvest the following year. Drums and sticks were used to beat away the evil spirits, songs were sung, and toast dipped in cider was put in the tree for the dryads before the wassail cup was passed around. Wassail originates from Saxon times and means "good health." It has pagan roots and is continued today in the Celtic tradition, but, sadly, only in a very few rural pockets of the Celtic lands. If you would like to keep this ancient practice alive and would enjoy taking part in a Wassailing ceremony, you can find out more from most Celtic Societies.

For the offering to the good spirits you will need:

1 piece of toast

(makes 12 servings)

As the cider cup is an offering to the goddess, have thankfulness and gratitude in your heart while making it. Put all of the ingredients into a large pot and heat to boiling point, but do not allow to boil. Turn the heat down, and then leave the mixture to simmer for twenty minutes.

For the ceremony you will need:

1 quart / liter of cider
(or apple juice for a non-alcoholic choice)
3 cinnamon sticks, 1 teaspoon cloves
250ml sugar
slices of fresh ginger root (to taste)
1 cup / 250ml of gin (optional)

THE WASSAILING CEREMONY

Wrap a little packet for each person present. Put a small charm into one of the packets and leave the rest empty. Place them all in a container and pass it around for each person to take one. Whoever receives the charm is the chosen king or queen and is the one to pour the libation around the roots of the tree and to place a piece of toast onto a branch. The toast is for the good spirits (which used to be seen as robins). A crown of evergreen leaves and tendrils can be worn by the king or queen of this night.

Beat sticks and drums to symbolically beat away the bad spirits. The king or queen should then pour the first cider from the wassail bowl in a clock-wise circle around the roots of the oldest or largest tree and place the toast in the tree. The wassail cup can then be passed around the group to share together. Let merriment abound, but do not forget that this is a cere-mony and not an opportunity to get drunk.

A traditional wassailing song is then sung. I have included my own version.

LEFT *The ancient Wassailing ceremony honors the old ways of giving as well as receiving.*

RIGHT *The ceremony iself is a time for thanks and sharing.*

"Hail and well met are we this night,
filled with the goddess of warmth and light.
Praise be to her for seed and grain,
thanks be to her for earth and rain.
Blessed be the spirit of the tree
For all her fruits − blessed be.
Blessed be."

RESOURCES

SALLY MORNINGSTAR Dip. V.Med. ITEC
PO Box 2633
Radstock
Bath BA3 5XR England
email sally.morningstar@talk21.com
*High Magic, shamanics, spiritual guidance, pain
relief, gem and flower essence consultations,
courses, and workshops. Mail-order catalogue
of shamanic essences and magical crafts.
Accepts commissions for magical crafts similar
to those featured in this book.*

INCENSE MAGIC
23 Baugh Gardens
Downend
Bristol BS16 6PN England
email insencemagic@saqnet.co.uk
*Magical and medicinal herbs, oils,
tinctures, and incense ingredients.*

FRED ALDOUS
PO Box 135
37 Lever Street
Manchester M1 1LW England
Tel: +44 (0)161-236 4224
Suppliers of hoops, raffia, and other craft materials.

THE INTERNATIONAL FLOWER
ESSENCE REPERTOIRE (IFER)
The Living Tree
Milland
Nr. Liphook
Hants GU30 7JS England
Tel: +44 (0)1428 741572
*Suppliers of flower and crystal
essences from around the world.*

WITCHES MOON
12 Gray Close
Innsworth
Glos. GL3 1EE England
email: witchesmoon@zetnet.co.uk
*Suppliers of
annual lunar
charts.*

BIBLIOGRAPHY

A MODERN HERBAL, *Mrs. M. Grieve,*
Penguin, UK, 1982

THE WOMAN'S DICTIONARY OF
SYMBOLS AND SACRED OBJECTS,
Barbara G. Walker,
Harper, San Fransisco, US, 1998

BREWERS BOOK OF MYTH
AND LEGEND, Helicon, UK, 1997

MAGICAL AROMATHERAPY,
Scott Cunningham, Llewellyn, US, 1996

MAGICAL HERBALISM,
Scott Cunningham, Llewellyn, US, 1995

MOON MAGICK,
D.J. Conway, Llewellyn, US, 1995

THE COMPLETE BOOK
OF AMULETS AND TALISMANS,
Migene Gonzalez Wippler, Llewellyn, US, 1997

THE COMPLETE BOOK
OF INCENSE OILS AND BREWS,
Scott Cunningham, Llewellyn, US, 1998

THE COMPLETE BOOK OF SPELLS,
CEREMONIES AND MAGIC,
Migene Gonzalez Wippler, Llewellyn, US, 1997

THE ENCYCLOPEDIA OF
FLOWER REMEDIES,
Clare G. Harvey and Amanda Cochrane, UK, 1995

THE MAGICIAN'S COMPANION,
Bill Whitcomb, US, 1998

WYLUNDT'S BOOK OF INCENSE,
Weiser, US, 1996

INDEX